Stan Toler's Practical Guide for Ministry Transition

How to Navigate Pastoral Change Personally and Professionally

Stan Toler

wesleyan publishing house
Indianapolis, Indiana

Published by Wesleyan Publishing House
Indianapolis, Indiana 46250
Printed in the United States of America
ISBN: 978-0-89827-385-4

Library of Congress Cataloging-in-Publication Data

Toler, Stan.
Stan Toler's practical guide for ministry transition : how to navigate pastoral change personally and professionally / Stan Toler.
p. cm.
Includes bibliographical references (p.).
ISBN 978-0-89827-385-4
1. Clergy--Relocation. I. Title. II. Title: Practical guide for ministry transition.
BV664.T65 2010
253'.2--dc22
2009051030

To Dr. Elmer L. Towns, my friend and
mentor since college days.

John C. Maxwell and I will never forget the day you came to Lancaster, Ohio, and taught our leadership team at Faith Memorial. Your message was life impacting, and your friendship over these years has been life changing for me. You are a brother beloved.

CONTENTS

Preface

This book is now the fourth in a series of practical guides for pastors, and I believe that you will find it uniquely useful at the time when you need it.

Nearly every pastor experiences a transition at some point in ministry. Sometimes the transition can be anticipated several weeks or months ahead of time. Other times it thrusts itself upon the pastor at a most unexpected and inopportune time. Whether planned or unplanned, this guide will help you sort through the issues you may face in your next pastoral transition.

There is so much to think about when it comes to leaving one ministry behind and looking ahead to the next. Conscientious pastors will want to leave their current congregation in the best shape possible and adequately prepare the leadership for the interim period between pastors. At the same time, you'll want to be preparing yourself and your family for the major changes that are to come in your life. Add to that the anxiety that is often felt about whether you are doing the right thing and how it will impact your children or other family members, and pastoral transition ends up at or near the most stressful times a pastor will ever face. This guide is designed to walk with you step by step through that process.

When it comes to ministry, I like to say, "It's not about theory, it's about practice." So in addition to key principles and big ideas, my goal is to give you lots of nuts-and-bolts tools you can use to make a smooth and effective transition to your next ministry post.

Transitioning from one ministry to the next is a wild ride, but one you can manage. After forty years of pastoral ministry, on July 3, 2009, a huge transition took place in my life. I was elected the thirty-ninth General Superintendent of the Church of the Nazarene. Talk about transition! I'm grateful to serve as your companion on the journey. Together we can do it!

STAN TOLER

ACKNOWLEDGMENTS

Many thanks to the team at Wesleyan Publishing House, especially Don Cady, Kevin Scott, Joe Jackson, Rachael Stevenson, and Lyn Rayn. Thanks also to Ron McClung for editorial assistance. Thank you for helping me elevate this project to a new level.

1

DISCERNMENT
Knowing When to Move

Not moving too soon and not staying too long require discernment.

If God wants to call me to a particular church,
he'll make sure it finds me.
—ED BRATCHER

Somewhere in the rainforests of Ecuador in 1956, five courageous missionaries—Jim Elliot, Nate Saint, Ed McCully, Peter Fleming, and Roger Youderian—were attacked and martyred by the very tribe they were attempting to reach with the gospel: the Huaorani or Auca Indians.

Several years later, sitting in a comfortable conference room, Pastor John listened as one of the missionaries' widows, Elisabeth Elliot, talked about deciding that she and her children would remain in Ecuador for awhile after her husband's death. To live in the vicinity of the very people responsible for her husband's martyrdom seemed like sheer folly at times. She often prayed, "Lord, what am I doing here?"

She heard him say, "You're here because I called you here, and I have not yet told you to leave."

That statement reverberated in Pastor John's mind and heart. He had been wondering recently why he was still in Plainville. It wasn't much fun anymore. In the five years he had been there, more than fifty people had joined the church. It wasn't phenomenal, but it was growth. The problem was that he had also conducted fifty funerals. Net growth: zero.

Added to that were the financial stresses. Several members had lost their jobs—some through downsizing and others the result of a downturn in the economy. The negative impact on the church coffers had brought serious tension to board meetings.

A popular staff member had felt led to move on to another assignment, creating a vacancy John had not yet been able to fill.

Maybe it was time for John to leave too? He certainly wasn't enjoying ministry anymore. The excitement was gone. He still enjoyed preaching, counseling, and caring for the flock, but much of his enthusiasm had drained away.

Still, what God had told Elisabeth Elliot, he also seemed to be saying to John: "You're here because I called you here, and I have not yet told you to leave."

The impact of those words touched him at a very deep level. John sensed God's presence in that conference room in a way he had not experienced for a long time.

Feeling a renewed sense of submission to God's plan, John lifted his heart in prayer. "All right, Lord," he said, sighing, "I'm here for the duration. Until you call me to do something else, I will persevere in Plainville."

It's one thing to make a commitment at a conference. It's another to maintain that commitment in the heat of the battle. John's decision to stay for the duration was about to be tested.

When *Not* to Move

Everybody experiences transition from time to time. You don't have to be in ministry to face change and to struggle with its implications. Engineers face transition. So do doctors, school teachers, and plumbers. People who work in government know their jobs are on the line when a new party comes to power.

Michael Griffin, administrator for the National Aeronautics and Space Administration (NASA), fully expected President Barack Obama to replace him once Obama took office. However, his wife, Rebecca, was not quite ready to accept the inevitable. On Christmas Eve 2008, she sent an e-mail to family and friends, asking them to sign an online petition, requesting President-elect Obama to retain her husband as NASA administrator.

Paul Light, a professor of public policy and presidential transition expert at New York University, joked, "It sounds like the only thing left is to stencil Mike Griffin on the side of [the] shuttle. . . . I've never heard of a campaign to keep one's job that goes beyond the edge of private discussion."[1]

Apparently Rebecca Griffin felt that desperate times called for desperate measures. However, before you arm your spouse with clipboard, pen, and petition in an effort to save your job, you should know that this method did not work for the Griffins. In the spring of 2009, President Obama appointed former shuttle commander and Vietnam veteran Charles Bolden to lead the space agency. Meanwhile, Griffin headed to the University of Alabama Huntsville to teach and conduct research.

Ministers who serve in denominations that appoint their pastors with minimal input from the congregations may feel, as Griffin did, at the mercy of their superiors. I have known of denominational supervisors who moved pastors from one parish to another, not based on the pastors' performance, good or bad, but on the whims of political forces within their congregations.

Most readers are likely serving in a church that "calls" its pastor. There may be denominational hoops to jump through to gain final approval, but the decision is generally an agreement between the congregation and the pastor.

So, assuming you have something to say about the decision, how can you discern when it's time to move and when it's time to stay put? Here are several inadequate reasons to move.

Discouragement

Avoid making the decision to move when your emotions are at low ebb. A Monday morning after a poorly attended service on a holiday weekend is not the best time to write your letter of resignation. Remember that another Sunday is coming. Chances are things will look better in a week or so.

Maybe instead of a disappointing Sunday, you're discouraged because you feel ineffective. Or perhaps the church, along with the rest of the world, is going through a financial downturn. Whatever the cause, it is all too easy for discouragement to trigger a pastor to think seriously about moving. As one pastor said, "I know churches everywhere have problems. But I'm ready to see some new faces on the problems."

Maybe it really *is* time to start over somewhere else. Just be sure you don't make the decision to move during a time of deep discouragement.

> **When to Make a Major Decision**
>
> "I would seek to remember not to get off the train when I'm going through the tunnel. There are plenty of discouragements in ministry, but it is not good to make a major decision during times of discouragement."
>
> —John Drescher[2]

Criticism

When a pastor is plagued by criticism, the result can be devastating. Severe criticism has led more than one minister to contemplate leaving. The plain truth is that anyone in a position of prominence will receive more than his or her fair share of criticism.

When Karl Rove was deputy White House Chief of Staff for President George W. Bush, he received frequent criticism for his advice to the president. Rove commented, "I'm an idiot one day and a genius the next—that's the way it is. You can't pay attention to that."[3]

Critics also abounded during the presidency of John Quincy Adams. For example, Adams' enemies accused him of providing an American girl for the Russian czar's sexual pleasure when he was minister to Russia. The claim was false, but this did not stop his detractors from spreading it around.[4]

Abraham Lincoln was the target for enormous criticism, and his perspective is worth considering: "If I were to try to read, much less answer, all the attacks made on me, this shop might as well be closed for any other business. I do the very best I know how—the very best I can; and I mean to keep doing so until the end." He continued, "If the end brings me out all right, what's said against me won't amount to anything. If the end brings me out wrong, ten angels swearing I was right would make no difference."[5]

Criticism is a fact of life for anyone in a leadership position, and so, in itself, it is never a sufficient reason to contemplate leaving a church.

Unresolved Conflict

Even pastors who develop a thick skin in regard to criticism can be tempted to leave when the church is embroiled in a major conflict. It's often much easier to cut and run than to stay and work through such a conflict.

A story floated around some time ago about the practice of a Jewish congregation at a synagogue in Eastern Europe. When the *shema* prayer (which comes from Deut. 6:4) was said, half the congregants stood and the other half remained seated. Those who were standing urged those who were sitting to stand up. Those who were seated urged those who were standing to sit down.

The rabbi did not know how to resolve this conflict, so he visited a ninety-eight-year-old man, one of the original founders of the synagogue, in a nursing home. The old man affirmed that standing during the prayer was not their tradition. Neither was sitting down.

"But," protested the rabbi, "the congregants fight all the time, yelling at each other about whether they should sit or stand."

The old man said, "*That* is our tradition!"[6]

I'm afraid it's the tradition in far too many congregations. As Jeff Mansell points out, "This is a trustworthy saying,

'Where two or more are gathered together, the possibility of conflict exists.'"[7]

If conflict is inevitable—and as long as we deal with human beings, it is—it is not a sufficient reason for leaving.

How Paul Decided When and Where to Move

When it comes to making a move, many of us are like Peter in the fishing boat, teetering on the edge of decision about stepping out. Wondering, like the fisherman, whether to stay in the boat or to step into the unknown, we say, "Lord, if it's you . . . tell me to come" (Matt. 14:28). But often we do not receive an immediate, clear word from the Lord beckoning us to a new assignment.

Pastors have long identified with the apostle Paul when it comes to making decisions, especially about where to serve at a given time. For much of his ministry, Paul was an itinerant preacher who traveled across the Mediterranean world—evangelizing, teaching, making tents to pay the bills, appointing local leaders, and then moving on to the next place.

Discerning the Right Time and Place

How did Paul decide the next destination and place of ministry on his missionary journeys? In truth, he did not always make the decision himself. Sometimes his opponents inadvertently made the decision for him. At Iconium, for instance,

> The people of the city were divided; some sided with the Jews, others with the apostles. There was a plot afoot among the Gentiles and Jews, together with their leaders,

> to mistreat them and stone them. But they found out about it and fled to the Lycaonian cities of Lystra and Derbe and to the surrounding country, where they continued to preach the good news. (Acts 14:4–7)

Like the pastor who learns of the secret board meeting on "how to get rid of the pastor," Paul saw the handwriting on the wall at Iconium and wisely called U-Haul. So, in this case, the time to move was before the death threat became reality, and the place was the nearest city of refuge.

On other occasions, Paul had very specific ideas about where to preach next. Having traveled through the regions of Phrygia and Galatia, he had a strong desire to preach in Asia, or what we would call Asia Minor. This province contained many important cities, with its capital Ephesus the finest and most populous. But the missionary party was "kept by the Holy Spirit from preaching the word in the province of Asia" (Acts 16:6). Just how they were forbidden, we do not know.

It would seem on the surface that Paul's logic was sound. He had planted churches in Derbe, Lystra, and Iconium, and later made another pass through each city, strengthening the churches. Now it seemed logical to turn to the great metropolitan centers of that region—such as Ephesus. Paul loved to be where the action was. So why did the Holy Spirit keep his team from going there?

When God Closes Doors

Bible scholars have suggested a number of reasons. Perhaps the timing wasn't right. Possibly God had someone else in mind for that mission. Maybe, for whatever reason, it was critical to establish churches in Macedonia first. As you may have noticed, God is not required to supply all of his reasons.

Some scholars have suggested that it was necessary for Priscilla and Aquila to prepare the way before Paul ministered in Ephesus. After his Macedonian ministry, the apostle met them in Corinth and accompanied them to Ephesus for a very brief visit. Leaving them there, he returned to his home base in Antioch before returning to Ephesus several months later. This time he stayed more than two years and had a marvelous ministry of teaching and healing.

The Spirit Trusts Us

"When our purpose and long-range goals are clear, we can dare to trust our consecrated thinking and responses of our emotions. The Spirit trusts us more than we trust Him at times."

—Lloyd Ogilvie[8]

So while we do not know why Paul could not minister in Asia Minor and Ephesus when he first wanted to do so, we can be confident that he was obedient to the Spirit's leading. When the Spirit said no, Paul did not keep beating on that door, trying to force the issue. He did the right thing by cooperating with the Spirit's plans.

With the door closed to Asia and Ephesus, Paul turned his attention to Bithynia, an area along the Black Sea, also containing many important cities. But in this case, "the Spirit of Jesus would not allow them to" go there either (Acts 16:7). However, after turning west and coming to the city of Troas, "Paul had a vision of a man of Macedonia standing and begging him, 'Come over to Macedonia and help us.'" Dr. Luke, who accompanied the apostle, reports, "After Paul had seen the vision, we got ready at once to leave for Macedonia, concluding that God had called us to preach the gospel to them" (Acts 16:9–10).

By going to Macedonia, Paul and his team established a beachhead for the gospel on the continent of Europe. As G. Campbell Morgan proposes, it may be that an "invasion of Europe was not in the mind of Paul, but it was evidently in the mind of the Spirit."[9]

God's Way Is Best

How did the Holy Spirit make it clear what Paul should do? Except in the case of the Macedonian vision, we cannot say for sure. We know Paul did not sit waiting for inspiration to strike him. He made plans to go to Asia and Ephesus. When that didn't work, he headed for Bithynia. When that plan fizzled, he trekked on to Troas. When one door closed, Paul simply headed for what might be the next open door. When it closed, he chose another alternative.

Subject to God's Will

"Man can always afford to lay his plans aside in deference to the divine will. It is wise that he should plan, but his plans must always be subject to alteration by the will of God."

—Charles Carter[10]

Hopefully, we will never get away from the idea that God still has a plan for his ministers. We are better off to go where God wants us to go, even if we don't understand his leading at first, than to stay when God has told us we should leave. On the other hand, if God has not given clear direction, it honors him when we pray, seek his face, and depend on the leadership of the Holy Spirit.

Recognizing the Signs

When deciding if it is time to move, we face external factors as well as internal factors. We mentioned some of the internal factors earlier: discouragement, criticism, and conflict. Other internal factors are a feeling of restlessness, a loss of enthusiasm, and a sense that you have taken a congregation as far as you can. Let's face it: A pastor may be quite capable of building a church from one hundred fifty to three hundred attendees, but have neither the skills nor the disposition to grow the congregation beyond that point.

Outside factors may include a telephone call from another congregation or a denominational official with an inquiry about whether you are willing to consider a different church. Here are a number of signs that it might be time for you to consider transitioning into a new ministry.

A Growing Desire for Change

Pastor Jim tells about serving his first congregation for a few years but feeling he had hit a brick wall in terms of effectiveness. Having gotten his feet wet as a solo pastor in a small church, he had a growing desire to work with young people and with music. Within a month or two of expressing this to his wife, the senior pastor of a medium-sized church three hundred miles away called to tell him he was looking for a minister of youth and music. Was he interested? Jim told him he would pray about it. When he got off the phone, he told his wife to pack while he prayed! It was the answer to his dream.

To be fair, Jim did pray about it. It didn't take long to feel positive about going for the interview, because the desire was already alive in Jim's heart to do the very thing they needed.

A Growing Conviction

Pastor Ted told about receiving a phone call from a denominational supervisor to consider a church in another state. The church was 20 percent larger than the congregation he was already serving, was located near a large university, and represented a chance to stretch himself beyond what he had done up to that time.

"Why do you think I would be well suited to pastor that congregation?" he asked. The executive immediately ticked off five reasons why it was a good fit.

To complicate matters, Ted could think of four or five good reasons to stay where he was. His family was established in the area, his influence had grown far beyond his congregation, his wife's aging parents lived nearby, he really had no good reason to leave his present church, and his wife loved the job she had in the community.

He promised the executive he would pray about it over the weekend. Early the next week, they talked again and he had no clear conviction one way or the other. Would he be willing to send a resume? He decided he would.

Then, a call from a congregational leader resulted in a telephone interview that lasted a couple of hours. That led to an invitation to visit the church, not as a candidate, but just to explore the possibilities. No announcement was made to the congregation that he was coming. Ted and his wife attended the worship service as visitors and were not publicly recognized. However, over the course of the weekend, they met with the church's governing board and had other meetings with church leaders.

The weekend went well, so the board asked him to return as a candidate. This time he preached and met with more groups of leaders. By the end of the weekend, the leaders were ready to recommend him to the congregation. They announced a congregational vote, which resulted in a strong positive call for him to come as their pastor.

The whole process took a few months. No one felt rushed to make a decision. But over time, Ted developed a growing conviction that the new church was where he was supposed to be. He gradually felt an inner release from responsibility from his current church.

Damaged Reputation

The previous two examples are positive factors. However, many pastors need to move on because of negative factors. Pastor Frank, in the interest of transparency, had a tendency to say too much publicly about his relationship with his wife. Before long, people became uncomfortable when he stood in the pulpit. What would he say today? How would he embarrass his family? How would he make the congregation feel uneasy?

A kind but firm lay leader met Frank for breakfast. "Pastor, I'm sorry to say you have damaged your credibility beyond repair. People start squirming in their seats because they're afraid of what you're going to say next."

The lay leader suggested it was time for Frank and his wife to move on to a different church. "I will give you a positive reference, because you and your wife are both gifted people. You need to begin afresh somewhere else. You need to learn from the mistakes you have made here and not repeat them in your next parish."

Betrayed Confidence

Pastor Sam's wife, Karen, developed a close friendship with Susan, one of the women in the church. Over coffee one afternoon, Karen confessed that she and Sam struggled with some aspects of their marriage. She revealed intimate details of their relationship. It was more than Susan could take. She and her husband left the church, because she "could not sit under *that man's* ministry any longer."

Things went from bad to worse, and Pastor Sam eventually resigned. He took a secular job for awhile as he and Karen worked on their relationship.

These examples (none are their real names) illustrate the fact that there is no single way to determine when to leave a church. In the first case, the young pastor had already developed a desire to do something different before the call came. In the second, a more seasoned pastor received a call "out of the blue."

Frank and Sam are not the first, nor will they be the last, pastors to get themselves into hot water because of indiscreet comments or ill-advised behavior. And we haven't even scratched the surface of pastors who leave because of organized opposition in the congregation.

We must acknowledge that forces sometimes militate against the pastor, and he or she loses control of the decision whether to stay or go. But let's think about some specific ways to nail it down: How can a pastor know it's time to leave?

Knowing When It's Time to Move On

Moving from one church to another is a huge decision. When a pastor makes the decision to leave without being pressured to do so by the congregation, people often misunderstand. They think the pastor is unhappy with them. They suspect she's looking for more money. If the pastor moves to a larger church, they may think he's just climbing the ecclesiastical ladder.

While you can't always control the perceptions of others, you always want to be sure you're leaving for the right reason. Here are a number of clear indicators that it is time to move on to another congregation.

When Your Vision Does Not Align with that of the Congregation

When you realize your vision for ministry does not match the church you're leading, it's probably time to leave. In the example above, Pastor Jim felt he was bashing his head against a wall. Although he tried, he had not been able to bring the congregation to the point of sharing his vision. Too entrenched in their comfortable ways, they could not get excited about bringing new people into the church. Meanwhile, Jim had found young people to be responsive. His love for worship music, along with his talent and skill, led him to desire a ministry that was different from the small church he led.

As it ended up, he did not serve as a long-term youth pastor, but his new church gave him plenty of opportunities to grow and stretch. He honed his skills at leading people to Christ in a church that welcomed new people. That youth and music assignment, though it lasted less than four years, prepared him for the next solo pastorate in which he proved to be extremely effective.

When Your Effectiveness Runs Dry

When you are no longer effective in your current parish, it may be time to move. Earlier, I mentioned a pastor who could lead a church from one hundred fifty to three hundred attendees but could go no further. The skills to grow a larger church are different than the skills it takes to arrive at that threshold. Corporate America has led us think our next job must always be bigger and better than the last. But there is no shame in handing off a healthy church to the next pastor and then going to a new assignment that may require the very skills that have proved to be effective for you.

Things You Cannot Do

You cannot be effective in everything. Things you cannot do:

- Control anyone or everything
- Change people or "fix" them
- Explain everything that happens
- Meet most people's expectations
- Avoid tough decisions
- Worry about who gets credit for what
- Cling to the past
- Do the ministry alone

—Chuck Swindoll[11]

I have known church planters who make lousy pastors. They excel at laying a new foundation, winning people to Jesus, and launching a church. But they are not effective in discipling people, administering a larger parish, or supervising staff. If the church grows to one hundred fifty people, it plateaus under their leadership. Such pastors should do what they're gifted to do—plant churches.

When You Feel a Sense of Release

When you sense God is releasing you from your current responsibilities, it may be time to leave. I have known colleagues who felt a sense of restlessness and could not put their finger on the cause. They had an inner sense that involvement in their current assignment was nearing an end. They weren't upset with anyone and no one was upset with them. The work was going reasonably well. From the outside, no one would guess there was a reason to leave. But the leader felt more and more it was time to move on to the next phase of ministry.

Intuition Is . . .

"Seeing the invisible . . .
Hearing the inaudible . . .
Testing the nonexistent . . .
And being able to
connect all of the dots!"
—Bobb Biehl[12]

When we talk about a feeling of restlessness, we're getting into an area that is difficult to define. Some would insist it is one way God leads us by his Spirit. Others might call it intuition. Still others might say it is a gut feeling. Whatever it is, we need to learn to trust it.

When You Have an Intuition

We often overlook or dismiss the value of intuition as a valid approach to decision-making because it does not rely on hard facts and empirical data. Yet often our gut instinct is important, because it reminds us how we genuinely feel about a matter.

Bob Kobielush points out that researchers have shown it is neither "brute rationality nor pure gut inspiration" that makes the right decision all the time. Rather they believe "the best approach is somewhere in between, and that the more complex or chaotic the situation, 'intuition usually beats rational analysis.'"[13]

So whether you begin to see that your vision no longer matches the congregation; you sense a drop in your effectiveness; you become aware of a feeling of restless anticipation about what's next; or you are fortunate enough to have someone calling you with an offer you have to consider; don't overlook the vital ingredients of intuition, prayer, seeking the will of God, and even counseling with trusted friends.

Staying For the Duration

After hearing Elisabeth Elliot speak, Pastor John returned home from the conference ready to tackle his responsibilities with new energy. If he was going to stay for the duration, he would do his very best to be effective.

A month later, his phone rang. It was a denominational supervisor in another state. Would he be interested in looking at a church similar in size to the one he was already serving? From the official's description of the congregation and its community, he knew that it would be an ideal fit for his gifts and ministry interests. It was an offer he had to consider.

John and his wife went for the interview. Although a big leap—geographically and culturally—they decided to make it. Looking back, he was amazed at God's timing. Thinking he was trapped in a church he no longer enjoyed, he could not imagine at the time moving to a church that turned out to be a great fit. But even more than that, he knew he had moved for the right reason. Because he had promised God he would stay for the duration, he knew he had not made the decision to move out of frustration or desperation.

When you're not sure what to do, hold steady. God is not the author of confusion. He will make it clear in his time.

Action Steps

1. List your current frustrations, discouragements, or unresolved conflicts. Beyond leaving, list other alternatives for dealing with these situations.

2. Analyze how the Holy Spirit has led you in the past. Do you feel any of those methods are currently at work? In what way?
3. On a scale of one to ten, with one being no comparison and ten being a perfect match, rate the following possibilities for considering it is time to move:
   - ___ Your vision does not match that of the congregation.
   - ___ Your effectiveness has run dry.
   - ___ You feel a sense of release.
   - ___ Your intuition tells you it is time for a change.

2

Perception
Seeing Greener Grass for What It Is

Declaring the grass is greener on the other side requires you to denigrate your own side of the fence.

The grass is always greener over the septic tank.
—Erma Bombeck

Parker Palmer, a prominent educator, was offered the opportunity to be president of a respected educational institution. Being a committed Quaker, he sought the help of what Quakers call a "clearness committee." He met with half a dozen friends who would ask questions designed to make God's will clearer in this matter.

Palmer later confessed in his book *Let Your Life Speak*, his real motive in calling the group together was not to discern anything about the position. He simply wanted to boast about a job he had already decided to accept.

During the course of the meeting, his friends asked a number of easy questions about his vision for the institution and its mission. Then someone asked a question that was rather penetrating: "Parker, what would you like about being president?"

After a thoughtful pause, he answered that he would not like all the fund-raising involved in the job. He would not like the politics, nor would he like giving up his study and teaching.

The questioner reminded him that the query was about what he would like, not what he would dislike.

Irritated by the reminder, he continued by saying he would not like giving up his summer vacation.

The third time the committee brought him back to the real question, he gave an honest answer, even though he was appalled by his own response: "I guess what I'd like most is getting my picture in the paper with the word *president* under it."

Instead of laughing, as he expected they would, the committee became quiet, while Parker began to sweat and inwardly groan.

Finally the questioner asked a question that did make everyone laugh: "Parker, can you think of an easier way to get your picture in the paper?"[1]

For Parker Palmer, the grass looked greener on the other side until his friends helped him face his real motivation. Many pastors have looked at other churches, other cities, other opportunities, assuming the grass was greener over there, only to discover, as Larry Osborne observed, that it was "only painted."[2] In other words, there's a reason why things look so good, and it may not always be positive.

Why the Other Grass Looks Greener

To be sure, sometimes the grass is greener. Sometimes the other church is a better situation, and it's appropriate to consider it.

But to keep from being fooled by appearances, we always need to think things through.

We also need to be aware of some reasons why pastors are vulnerable to the *greener-grass syndrome*. Why are other fields tempting to us? See if any of these reasons sound familiar.

Unwise Comparisons

If you have ever been to a ministerial meeting where pastors are talking about how many people were in church last Sunday, or how many people prayed to receive Christ last month, or how their offerings are growing, you know what I'm talking about. There's always someone who is better off than you are. There's always a bigger and better situation across town, upstate, or across the country.

> **Unwise Comparisons**
>
> "Too many of us gauge our self-worth and significance by using those around us as a benchmark. The advertising industry capitalizes on our weakness by offering a steady stream of dream homes, thin waistlines and sporty SUVs."
>
> —Todd Gaddis[3]

Even the pastors of super churches feel the pull to bigger and better things. Keith Drury wrote a column in the mid 1990s, around the time three well-known pastors of large churches left their pulpits to pursue other opportunities.[4] Drury mused about why Chuck Swindoll would leave his church in Fullerton, California, to become president of Dallas Theological Seminary; why John Maxwell would leave Skyline Wesleyan Church in the San Diego area to devote full time to his INJOY organization, moving it to Atlanta; and why Dale Galloway would leave his church in Portland, Oregon, to take a position at Asbury Theological Seminary in

Wilmore, Kentucky. Was it greener pastures that tempted these successful pastors to leave at what some might call the peak of their careers?

Drury does not mention greener pastures, but he does suggest a number of reasons why people at this stage in their pastoral careers might consider making a change. For example, being pastor of a super church is simply hard work. Also, each of these men had passed his fiftieth birthday when he made his move. Other possible reasons he cites include the daily grind of leading a large, complex church; the sense that things are not moving fast enough; and the reality that the pastor's vision is outpacing the church's progress. Maybe God even told them to change.

My purpose in pointing out these super-church pastors, who were considered highly successful, is not to question their motives for moving on, but to point out that no matter what level you achieve in life, there is always something bigger or better or more challenging. Making comparisons can leave you feeling the grass is greener elsewhere.

Understanding the unfruitfulness of such comparisons is a good step toward stopping the practice. So is calling such comparisons what they are. For Craig Brian Larson, the comparisons he made early in his ministry were actually envy. He coveted the success God had given to others. He learned to admit his error and not sugarcoat the practice. "To label my fever of relentless comparisons with as benign a term as the 'greener-grass syndrome' grossly missed the naked truth. My healing came when I called my feelings what they were."[5]

The Constant Grind

After a few years in the same place, a pastor begins to wonder, "What can I tell them that I haven't already said?" How can a pastor continue to be creative after preaching four Advent sermons every year for several years? Or Palm Sunday and Easter messages every year?

It often seems easier to make a fresh start somewhere else. The people in your current congregation have heard all your personal illustrations, but your sermon barrel is full, and the same messages would sound new and fresh in a different place.

This short-sighted approach, however, short-circuits the pastor's personal growth. Steward Pierson suggests that short pastoral tenures emphasize appearance and flash. On the other hand, long tenures "call us to probe the depths of our souls, where Christians believe Christ is uniquely present."[6]

Misunderstanding Success

Pastors often make false assumptions about success when they look across the fence at a greener pasture. First, they assume that ministry is easier in a "successful" church. It certainly looks easier. But remember that you probably haven't gotten close enough to see the blood, sweat, and tears of those in the trenches of that ministry. From twenty thousand feet in an airplane, I can't see the trash littering the highway, but in an automobile on the way from the airport, I may see that a cleanup crew is long overdue.

The other false assumption is that the success they've had in one setting can simply be transplanted to a new, greener setting. Pastors who leave one church and move to another may soon find out what worked in the previous parish does not work in the new place. People are different, the culture may be different, and the chemistry between pastor and people is different.

The Potential Trap

Most of us never approach our full potential, but once we decide to do our best to reach our God-given potential, we may subject ourselves to another trap—trying to achieve the impossible. The problem in ministry is there's always more to do. There are more mountains to climb, more people to help, more sermons to prepare, more problems to solve, and one more opportunity to seize.

Success

"Success is complex. In addition to the Holy Spirit, a host of factors contribute to an organization's success or failure. . . . Too often in church work, God gets the glory if it succeeds, and we pastors get the blame if it fails."

—Leith Anderson[7]

We will talk more about potential in the next chapter, but just a word of caution here: pursuing potential can result in following a "faulty compass, one that always points to the bigger platform, the larger ministry, and the more challenging task. It never suggests that we are in over our heads, that . . . God might want us to be still rather than charge ahead."[8]

Impatience

Another reason we are tempted to look at greener pastures is that we grow impatient. Many of us are like the pastor whose friend found him pacing in his study one day.

His friend asked, "Why all the agitation?"

"It's because I'm in a hurry and God is not," replied the impatient pastor.

It's easy to confuse movement with progress. Eugene Peterson has little patience with pastoral impatience, the kind that induces pastors to move to a new parish when the people they recruit in a local church don't produce. Restless pastors simply shake the dust off their feet and move on to a different location. In strong language, he writes, "Impatience, the refusal to *endure*, is to pastoral character what strip mining is to the land—a greedy rape of what can be gotten at the least cost, and then abandonment in search of another place to loot."[9]

Ouch! Lord, help us to endure.

The Greener Pastures

Nobody could blame the young man for the choices he had made. After all, he had started life at a disadvantage. His father died young, so his uncle took him under his wing.

The man's uncle was good to him, taking him along wherever he went. With no children of his own, he treated him like his own son. His uncle was also a religious man—he honored God faithfully and made it a practice to consult the Lord about major decisions.

When times turned hard and it became difficult to make a living on the farm, the man and his uncle decided to relocate, a move that proved favorable. His uncle's flocks and herds grew until he gained a reputation as a prosperous rancher.

But soon they ran into trouble. The big landowner in the area began making overtures toward Uncle's wife. The situation became tense, but finally Uncle cleared out, taking his wife and his nephew with him.

Once again, their relocation led to further prosperity. The man's uncle generously offered to let him start his own herd. Before long, the land was overflowing with all their livestock.

Sometimes quarrels broke out between his own hired hands and the men who worked for his uncle. Uncle finally said, "This is not right. I don't want a range war to break out between your men and mine. Look over the land. There's plenty of it. You take what you want and I'll take what's left."

You know the rest of the story. Lot saw the plain. It was lush with plenty of moisture. It reminded him of the land where they lived before the big guy with the roving eye—Pharaoh—forced them out. So Lot chose the greener pastures of Jordan, because they looked so much like Egypt. Uncle Abram took what was left. For Lot, the grass was literally greener on the east side, down toward the Jordan River, in close proximity to the cities of Sodom and Gomorrah.

Lot made his choices, but he did not become a governor or senator. He became a resident of Sodom, surrounded by wickedness of every unspeakable variety. Lot's progression of choices provides some important lessons on decision-making and greener grass. Lot based his decision on what he could see with his own eyes: "Lot looked up and saw that the whole plain of Jordan was well watered, like the garden of the Lord, like the land of Egypt" (Gen. 13:10). Then, in apparent disregard for Uncle Abram and his well-being, Lot selfishly chose what seemed best for him and his family: "So Lot chose for himself the whole plain of the Jordan . . . Abram lived in the land of Canaan, while Lot . . . pitched his tents near Sodom" (Gen. 13:11–12).

Lot used his power to choose, but it was an unfortunate choice: "Now the men of Sodom were wicked and were sinning greatly against the LORD" (Gen. 13:13). What a place to rear a family! Lot's unwise choices led to more unforeseen and unfortunate consequences. He lost his wife, and eventually "the old man succumbed to the scheming of his unscrupulous daughters,"[10] who led him into incestuous relations while he was drunk.

Unwise Comparisons

"Resolved: That all men should live for the glory of God. Resolved: That whether others do or not, I will."

—Jonathan Edwards[11]

This sad story reminds us that what looks greener on the other side does not always turn out to be the verdant Shangri-la we imagined it to be. We must be careful in making our choices, since one choice leads to another and soon the consequences are inevitable.

It is paramount in decision making that we keep the focus on God and his plan. Beyond that, we should strive to keep our wits about us, carefully investigate our options, and maintain a clear head about our motives; this will result in better decisions.

While Lot made decisions for greener pastures that led him further from God, Abram made decisions that brought him closer to God: "Abram moved his tents and went to live near the great trees of Mamre at Hebron, where he built an altar to the LORD" (Gen. 13:18). Consequently, we remember Abram for his faith, while we remember Lot for his folly.

Wading through the Greener Grass

To avoid making destructive decisions such as Lot made, we should attempt to learn as much as we can about the greener pastures of pastoral ministry before we leave behind the pasture where we currently serve. If another parish is looming large in your mind, and especially if someone has contacted you about a specific opportunity, how can you be sure it's the right one for you?

The Church and Its Community

How much do you know about the church you're considering and the community where it's located? What kind of people are members of the church? Yes, all God's children are important, but none of us is a good fit for every congregation.

If it's a rural church, even a growing, healthy one, and you've never even visited a farm, you'd better think twice. One denominational supervisor in the Midwest, when potential pastors contacted him about opportunities, would honestly tell them about a rural congregation, "It is thirty miles to the nearest McDonald's or Wal-Mart." Many quickly lost interest.

One day a pastor who had grown up on a farm called. Living so far from a town did not dissuade him. His wife would love to have room to plant a large flower garden and put in a few rows of vegetables. They were able to thrive on conditions that would drive many pastors and their families crazy.

Other questions to consider about a greener pastures parish include:

- How have the church's demographics changed in the past five years?
- Do church members live in the community or do they drive in from a distance?
- Is the community around the church changing or is it consistent and compatible with the people who attend there?
- What do future trends indicate?
- Are the homes near the church affordable for young families looking for housing?

None of these issues would necessarily be the deciding factor in determining whether it's really the right opportunity for you, but you need to know. How can you make an informed decision if you don't know?

The Church and Its Attitudes

What are the prevailing attitudes in the church? For example, what is their attitude about worship? Have they fought the worship wars? If so, who won?

What is their attitude about evangelism? Almost every church will tell you it wants to grow. Is there any evidence this church really means it?

One pastor, going through the interview process, asked the search committee, "Apart from hiring a new senior pastor, what are the things you would most like to accomplish in the coming year?" All the answers dealt with the church property—a new roof, a remodeling project, recoating the parking lots.

Inwardly, the pastoral candidate struggled over whether to point this out or to keep silent and move on to something else. He finally decided to risk saying what was on his mind. After a pause, he pointed out their answers all dealt with the physical properties.

"I was just wondering," he said, "if anyone is concerned about the people in this community who do not know Jesus."

It became very quiet for a few moments while the members of the committee scrambled to find a resolution the church board had passed a year or so earlier, calling for greater outreach. Finally, a man on the search committee said, "I really think we're waiting for someone to show us how to be more effective in reaching others."

The candidate took that as a positive sign, eventually accepted the call to be their pastor, and the church did have significant outreach in the years that followed.

What are the congregation's attitudes about racial or ethnic diversity? Are "all kinds of people" welcome in the church? Has the church ever participated in cooperative ministries that reached across boundaries to interact with churches of other races or ethnic groups?

What is the church's attitude toward its denomination or its supervisory body? If it is obligated to pay denominational budgets, what is its record of payment? Do they participate happily or begrudgingly?

The Church and Its Inner Workings

How do the people get along with each other? Who makes the decisions in the church? Is the decision-making process controlled by one family, one high-powered individual, or does the board function as representatives of the people? Have recent internal conflicts disrupted the congregation? Has the church experienced division in its recent history?

Why is the present pastor leaving? What about the pastor prior to this one? What is the church's history in pastoral relations?

This is not an exhaustive list of things you should know about a prospective church. But if you're thinking of making a major decision like changing churches, the more you know, the better prepared you are to make an informed decision. Reliable information is your friend. It is the antidote to falling ill with the greener-grass syndrome.

Reexamining the Grass on Your Side of the Fence

In addition to learning about the church of greener pastures, it always pays to take an honest look at your own grass, your own situation, and your own opportunities before you jump the fence. You may be looking at some weeds that have threatened to overtake the good grass on your own side of the fence. What are some things that can affect your vision?

The Weed of Personal Conflict

Have you recently been hurt? Good people can sometimes say hurtful things, remarks that cut deeply. As someone has pointed out, "Hurting people hurt people." We have a lot of hurting people in our world—people who have lost their jobs, lost their marriages, lost their kids, lost their self-esteem. In their own anger or anguish, they lash out at others, sometimes even those who try to help, like their pastor.

Are you tired of dealing with an irritating person? Every church has them. They rub you the wrong way. They stop by unannounced. They may say things like, "Pastor, I had a little time to kill so I thought I would stop by and see how you're doing."

One pastor wondered, "Why is it that people who have nothing to do want to do it with me?" People will often provide you with some great blessings, but they can also drain your energies.

I'm guessing the pastor in a cartoon I saw had been dealing with difficult people. It showed the pastor posting his sermon topic on the church bulletin board. The message said, "Just come and find out, Meathead!" Two parishioners are standing by and one of them says, "You can always tell when he needs a vacation."[12]

If you need a vacation, take it. But that doesn't necessarily mean you need to jump the fence to greener pastures. A wise pastor, who had been in his parish for ten years, had weathered some storm of personal conflict. He said, "You just gotta stay and work through this stuff. Otherwise you go somewhere else, take your baggage with you, and repeat the same mistakes. Or the church calls someone else and they go through the same thing with the next pastor. When you leave too soon, nobody learns anything."

The Weed of a Fading Call

How is your sense of call to your current parish? Is it still strong? Lynn Anderson told the story of a witch doctor, sitting at a fork in the road deep in the jungle. A traveler happened upon the scene and watched the witch doctor, deep in concentration while he tossed a stick repeatedly in the air.

"What are you doing?" the traveler asked.

The shaman answered, "I'm asking the medicine stick which way I am to go. As it falls to the ground it points the way."

"But why do you throw it so many times?" the traveler wanted to know.

"Because I don't want to go where the stick is pointing!"[13]

Has the stick repeatedly pointed toward staying where you are, and you're rebelling against it? Or is your call to remain still strong and you're embracing it?

The Weed of a Dying Dream

Is your dream still alive? A pastor is the chief dreamer for the church. He or she is the person who must cast a vision for where the church should go and what the church should be. Is your dream still vivid? Or is it fading in the glittering light of greener pastures?

Reality of a Dream

"Nothing is as real as a dream. The world can change around you, but your dream will not. Responsibilities need not erase it. Duties need not obscure it. Because the dream is within you, no one can take it away."

—Tom Clancy[14]

Bobb Biehl points out that dreams make a daily difference. "Without dreams," he says, "a person flops out of bed in the morning, drifts through the day and jumps into bed at night . . . frustrated at the lack of significant life progress. With dreams, a person jumps out of bed in the morning, focuses on priority next steps and flops into bed at night . . . thankful for any bit of progress towards the dream."[15]

The Weed of Cloudy Opportunities

Do you still see exciting opportunities where you are? Don't be too quick to say no. Ann Landers reminds us that "Opportunities are usually disguised as hard work, so most people don't recognize them."[16]

If you're tired, you may not even be looking for opportunities. The last thing you want is more hard work. But that may be a sign you need to rest, not jump the fence. We can become so immersed in what we're already doing that we really don't want to think about one more thing. An opportunity can look like a burden, not a challenge.

Reality of a Dream

"We typically see things, not as they are, but as we are. . . . Too often our minds are locked on one track. We are looking for red, so we overlook blue; we are thinking tomorrow, and God is saying now; we are looking everywhere, and the answer is under our nose."

—John Mason[17]

Just be sure, before you ride off to greener pastures, that you haven't left some great opportunity unexplored where you are.

The Greatest Enterprise

Parker Palmer did not take the job of college president. If he had, he probably would have experienced "fatigue, discouragement, a loss of joy, lack of energy, and a sense of inadequacy" in his new job.[18] He would have discovered the grass is not always greener on the other side. It just looks good for awhile.

Are you willing to pay the price to stay in your church? You may feel that you're working under a crushing burden right now. You may feel that you can't go on another day unless something changes. What if nothing changes? Are you willing to pay the price to stay?

To do this, of course, will mean to face your pain, reaffirm your commitment to bloom where you're planted, and press forward. If God wants you to move, then by all means move.

But, if God wants you to stay, great blessings may be waiting just over the horizon, because that's the payoff for staying put when the grass only looks greener somewhere else.

Action Steps

1. Analyze churches or pastors you're tempted to envy because they seem bigger, brighter, and more effective than you or your church. See if you can list some weaknesses "on the other side of the fence" as well as some strengths. Do this, not to be critical, but realizing that in every green patch of grass there are a few brown spots.
2. Write down the areas of conflict in your current parish. Discuss these with a trusted friend. Determine with your friend if they're worth pushing you to the other side of the fence.
3. What factors enticed you to come to your current church? What has changed?

3

POTENTIAL

Discovering Your Leadership Potential and Ministry Place

Before you transition to a new assignment, reflect on your potential and where God may be uniquely preparing you to serve.

Nothing is more common than unfulfilled potential.
—HOWARD HENDRICKS

When Jimmy Carter ran for president of the United States, the press—and the world—became thoroughly acquainted with his family, including his brother Billy. When Billy drank too much, he talked too much, made outrageous statements, and then later discovered his comments had been broadcast to the world through the media.

The irony of the situation, according to Jimmy, was that his mother considered Billy the smartest of her children. Billy read voraciously. In the pre-White House days, by the time Jimmy arrived at the warehouse each morning at six-thirty, Billy would have already devoured all four newspapers available in Plains, Georgia. Billy became a walking encyclopedia on subjects such as international affairs, American politics, and baseball. He would make what sounded like foolish comments to unsuspecting people, wager that he was right, and earn a lot of money when his statements proved to be factual.

During the presidential campaign of 1976, a reporter remarked to Billy that he seemed a little strange. He replied, "My mama was a seventy-year-old Peace Corps volunteer in India, one of my sisters goes all over the world as a holy-roller preacher, my oldest sister spends half her time on a Harley-Davidson motorcycle, and my brother thinks he's going to be president of the United States. Which one of our family do *you* think is normal?"

After the inaugural parade in January 1977, the Carter family left the reviewing stand and began to walk toward the White House. As expected, news reporters soon pressed in with their microphones. Jody Powell, Jimmy Carter's press secretary, told the family, "Now, don't anybody stop to answer their questions."

Carter's mother told Jody, "You might tell Jimmy what to do, but not the rest of us."

Reporters quickly surrounded her and asked, "Miss Lillian, aren't you proud of your son?"

While the new president waited for his mother to offer congratulatory words, she said, "Which one?"[1]

American history bulges with examples of people who exceeded expectations, like a peanut farmer, a rail splitter, and a community organizer, all of whom became U.S. presidents.

Thomas Edison's teachers told him he was too stupid to learn. He became a great inventor anyway.

When F. W. Woolworth was twenty-one years of age, his employer would not permit him to wait on customers at the store where he worked because, in the employer's opinion, the young man did not have enough sense. When Woolworth died in 1919, his retail corporation was worth sixty-five million dollars.

Lou Gehrig was asked to quit his boyhood team because he was such a poor player. He went on to play major league baseball, including a streak of 2,130 consecutive games, a record that stood for more than fifty years. He was inducted in the National Baseball Hall of Fame.

When Walt Disney submitted his first drawing, the editor told him he had absolutely no talent. He went on to build a great animation entertainment empire anyway.

What is your potential? What has God uniquely gifted you to do? To become? Are you finding and developing your potential?

How Much Potential Do We Have?

People who study the human family have suggested that human beings use a relatively small percentage of their potential, perhaps only 20 to 30 percent.[2] An anonymous wit observed, "The greatest undeveloped territory in the world lies under your hat."

Acknowledging that human beings may never reach 100 percent of their potential, why do we fall short? What's preventing us from taking more advantage of our capability?

Deep Wells of Strength

"Few men during their lifetime come anywhere near exhausting the resources dwelling within them. There are deep wells of strength that are never used."

—Admiral Richard E. Byrd[3]

Self-Imposed Limitations

Our greatest limitations are those we impose on ourselves. Roger Bannister's feat in running the mile in less than four minutes has become legendary. Prior to his accomplishment, many thought it was humanly impossible. Yet multiplied hundreds have done it since, crashing through what was once a mythical barrier. Today the world record is 3:43.13, which a Moroccan, Hicham el-Gerrouj, set in 1999. His record has stood for more than a decade. Has man finally reached his full potential as a runner, or will someone clip a few seconds off that pace in the years to come?

Similar stories could be repeated many times over as human beings surmount supposedly impossible barriers in all kinds of endeavors.

A pastor told me about a period in his ministry when he heard many negative voices in his church and he allowed them to influence him more than they should have. Consequently, he stopped growing, the church stopped growing, and both his potential and theirs remained unfulfilled. He was in a dark tunnel, spiritually and professionally. He felt trapped and it took a deep experience of spiritual insight to rise above it.

I admire pastors who see the limitations but refuse to allow artificial ceilings to define reality for them. They grow beyond the boundaries, both in personal growth and in church growth.

Failure to See Our Own Potential

The football coach walked into a hospital and took an elevator to the second floor. After asking directions at the nurses' station, he walked down the hallway toward the room with a solemn look on his face. He entered the room and moved toward the bandaged figure on the bed. The patient saw him, smiled wanly, and raised an arm from which tubes dangled.

"Thanks for coming, Coach."

"How are you doing?"

"Oh, okay," the patient said, although a mournful look in the sunken eyes told a different story.

After a long pause, the coach leaned in, his jaw jutting close to the face of the patient. He said, "Listen, Mike, I need you in training camp in July—on the field, ready to go. We're going all the way this year."

Later, Mike Westhoff recovered from bone cancer and continued his job as special teams coach for the Miami Dolphins. Concerning that experience in the hospital, he said about Coach Don Shula, "I thought he would tuck me in, but he didn't. He treated me the way I could be, not the way I was." Shula was thinking *potential*.[4]

Someone else may see your potential better than you can see it. Blessed are pastors whose mentors come alongside and, instead of coddling us and feeding our self-pity, challenge us with the potential in ourselves and in our opportunities.

Your Special Role

God expects every Christian "to discover and fulfill his special role in the context of the believing community. Once this is understood, the believer . . . will not aspire to be more than God intends him to be, but he will not settle for being less than he was created and redeemed to be."

—Stuart Briscoe[5]

Low Self-Esteem

Reasons abound as to why people develop low self-esteem. Some blame their parents, teachers, or coworkers. Wherever the blame lies, it's up to the individual to rise above it.

Perhaps you're wondering about the apostle Paul's caution not to think more highly of ourselves that we ought. Be sure you read the rest of what he says: "Do not think of yourself more highly than you ought, but rather think of yourself with sober judgment, in accordance with the measure of faith God has given you" (Rom. 12:3).

In short, we often fail to see ourselves as God sees us. Jesus said we must love our neighbors as we love ourselves (Luke 10:27). Someone observed, "That's our problem. We don't like ourselves very much and we treat everyone else accordingly."

The truth is, we have enormous potential. Paul Meyer said, "There isn't a ruler, a yard stick or a measuring tape in the entire world long enough to compute the strength and capabilities inside you."[6] But do you believe that? How can we serve an all-powerful, all-wise God and not believe it? After all, "With God all things are possible" (Matt. 19:26).

The Shepherd Boy with Potential

It was a sad day in Israel. Instead of following the prophet Samuel's instructions regarding the destruction of the Amalekites, King Saul decided to use his own judgment and discriminate between those he would spare and those he would not. He destroyed only the "despised and weak," while sparing King Agag and "the best of the sheep and cattle . . . everything that was good" (1 Sam. 15:9).

Saul the discriminate became Saul the disobedient, which soon led to Saul the arrogant, who "set up a monument in his own honor" (1 Sam. 15:12). The whole process sickened the Lord God, who became grieved that he had made Saul king (1 Sam. 15:10–11).

So where would God find a new leader for his people? He ignored Saul's descendants, disregarded Saul's closest advisors and military leaders, and instead sent Samuel to the town of

Bethlehem to find a man named Jesse. One of Jesse's sons had the potential to become king. Not the eldest son. Not the tallest. Not the most impressive. Rather, the youngest.

Who knew? Who knew the next king of Israel would come not from a palace or the ranks of the military, but from a sheep pasture?

Potential often hides behind strange garb. It surfaces when tested. In David's case, his potential may have remained hidden except for the bear that came into his flock and carried off a sheep. Many a shepherd, concerned with his own safety, would have sacrificed the sheep. Not David.

He pursued the bear. Untapped potential rose within him and gave him the courage to confront the animal. When it turned on him, he grabbed it by the hair, struck it, and killed it. Ursa Major became "Ursa Dead" at the hands of David (1 Sam. 17:34–37).

Who knew he could kill a bear barehanded? Or a lion? David himself did not know until he did it.

The confidence David gained from those successful defenses of his flock gave him the courage to face the giant Goliath. While his brothers and the other soldiers of Israel trembled in their sandals, David informed King Saul he was not afraid to fight the giant. In fact, he said, "The Lord who delivered me from the paw of the lion and the paw of the bear will deliver me from the hand of this Philistine" (1 Sam. 17:37).

Rejecting the offer of Saul's armor, David raced into the valley, armed only with his slingshot, his confidence in God, and five smooth stones—which proved to be four more than he needed. Ignoring the giant's taunts, David slung a stone at Goliath's bushy pate. Nothing like that had ever entered his head before! And nothing ever did again, because the giant crashed to

Self-Leadership

"Although self-leadership isn't talked about much, make no mistake, it is a good part of the ballgame. How effectively can any of us lead others if our spirits are sagging, our courage is wavering, and our vision or commitment is weak?"

—Bill Hybels[7]

the ground, and David killed him with the monster's own sword.

Who knew David had such potential? Not his brothers. Not his king. But David believed in himself and in his God. He transformed potential into power. And his potential grew.

It's one thing to rise to the occasion as an individual. But how do you motivate others? How do you lead an army to fulfill its potential? Not everyone who exhibits personal courage can bring out the same potential in others.

Sometime later, David gained the opportunity to prove his leadership potential. He and his men returned from battle only to discover that enemy soldiers had raided their campsite, burned their belongings, and carried off their women and children. His men, weary from their battles, were not only worried about their families, but angry with their leader. Their bitterness rose in their throats and some of them thought the best solution was to stone David.

How would David respond to this crisis? Could he turn their anger against him into anger against the enemy?

His first response was not to calm his men, soothe them, or try to persuade them. Instead, first he found strength in the Lord. Specifically, "David strengthened himself in the LORD his God" (1 Sam. 30:6 RSV).

When the crisis came, David was astute enough to know who needed leadership the most. It was not his men. It was himself.

Before we can lead others, we must lead ourselves. Finding and developing our potential is an internal issue.

David is not the only biblical character whose potential had to be discovered and developed. Matthew was a government employee who became an apostle. Gideon was a common laborer when God called him and equipped him to become a valiant leader of men. Jacob, the deceiver, became the person after whom the whole nation of Israel is named.

Deborah was a housewife when she became a judge in Israel. Moses had to overcome his stuttering to become the deliverer of God's people. Jeremiah was a child in his own eyes until God inspired him to speak the Word of the Lord. Nicodemus overcame his legalistic tendencies as a Pharisee in order to become a defender of the Christian faith. Joseph went from prisoner to prime minister. Esther, an orphan, ascended to the throne as queen. Abraham, a nomad, became the father of many nations. Mary, an unknown virgin, gave birth to the Son of God. Isaiah, a man of unclean lips, prophesied the birth of God's Messiah. God transformed Saul the persecutor into Paul the missionary, who wrote two-thirds of the New Testament.

John Mason, reflecting on such characters, observed, "All God needs to use you is all of you!"[8]

Factors for Peak Potential

Does he have all of you? Are you operating at peak performance?

Bill Hybels remembers a time when three wise people from his congregation came to him and reminded him of two eras during the first twenty years of Willow Creek Community Church's history when he was not at his leadership best. They told him, "The data shows Willow Creek paid dearly for your leadership fumble. It cost Willow more than you'll ever know when you were off—not hitting on all 8 cylinders."

They went on to tell him the best gift he could give to his church was "a healthy, energized, fully surrendered, focused self."[9]

In other words, they were telling him this was the only way he would ever reach his full potential and lead the church toward reaching its potential. The same is true for you and me.

What are some key ingredients in remaining focused? What will help us keep ourselves on track?

A Clear Calling

Citing 1 Corinthians 3:5—"The Lord has assigned to each his task"—Max Lucado suggests three questions to help us stay clear about our calling.[10]

In what directions has God taken you? Nobody else has had your precise career path. What does his direction suggest to you? A colleague told me all his churches have been "turn-around" situations, churches that had seen better days. Each needed revitalization and, in most cases, that is exactly what happened under his leadership. It argues for the idea that God is helping him fulfill his potential as a turnaround pastor.

What needs has God revealed to you? What breaks your heart? What causes you to weep? What gets you excited when it comes to meeting needs?

What abilities has God given to you? We all have them. What is it that you do well? In what areas do you excel?

The answers to these questions will help clarify your calling, which in turn keeps you on track toward fulfilling your potential.

A Focused Vision

When retail giant J. C. Penney was ninety-five years old, he said, "My eyesight may be getting weaker, but my vision is improving."[11]

That is so much better than those who die at age thirty and are buried at age seventy, spending more than half their lives in a somnambulistic (sleep-walking) state! People never become peak performers if their vision is unclear.

What do you see? What is the preferred future for your ministry and your church? What is your vision impelling you to do? Is your vision sharp and focused, or does it need a tune-up?

A Focused Vision

In college David Livingstone heard an address by the missionary Robert Moffat, who spoke of seeing in the mist of the morning the smoke of a hundred villages where the gospel had never been preached.[12] Those words sparked a vision in Livingstone that kept him focused enough to walk hundreds of miles up the Zambezi River through uncharted jungle.

A Glowing Passion

What warms your heart and propels you into action? Or have you become comfortable with the routine? Vance Havner said, "Too much of our orthodoxy is correct and sound, but like words without a tune, it does not glow and burn; it does not stir the heart; it has lost its hallelujah. One man with a genuine glowing experience with God is worth a library full of arguments."[13]

You are not likely to fulfill your potential until you "glow and burn" with the passion to reach others for Christ and to grow them in discipleship. As Abraham faced the perishing people of Sodom, he interceded on their behalf (Gen. 18). Is your passion motivating you to pray for the lost of your community?

People without passion become people whose potential lies unfulfilled. In fact, Howard Hendricks advised, "Don't put live eggs under dead chickens."[14] In other words, don't waste your opportunities on passionless people.

A Consistent Character

Before you can achieve worthwhile things and fulfill your potential, you must be a person of sterling character. Actions come from motives. And worthy motives arise from solid character. Before you can do, you must be.

Stephen Covey talks about the "inside-out approach," by which he means that good solutions, lasting agreements, and happiness that endures all come from inner greatness. "The inside-out approach says that private victories precede public victories, that making and keeping promises to ourselves precedes making and keeping promises to others." He goes on to declare that "it is futile to put personality ahead of character, to try to improve relationships with others before improving ourselves."[15]

An Ear Attuned to the Spirit

Are you listening to the voice of the Spirit in your inner consciousness? Or are you just plowing ahead, assuming (hoping) he will bless your efforts? You understand, don't you, that the best ideas—whether you're talking about sermon series or growth strategies—come from God. He knows your congregation and your community better than you do. He knows what the hot issues are, where the hurts are, and where the potential is.

As a young man, Everett Cattell struggled with his tongue. At parties he would be a lively conversationalist, but sometimes he went too far; he said too much. Not that he told off-color stories or falsehoods, but the lightness and silliness of his words sent him home with a feeling of emptiness. A conscientious Christian, he would pray and make up his mind not to say so much next time.

Yet if he sat in the corner and refused to participate, his friends would think something was wrong with him. Normally he was the life of the party, so people wondered why he was so quiet. They would urge him to participate and it wouldn't be long until he was laughing and talking, and, once again, talking a bit too much.

Finally, after one more negative experience with his tongue, he seemed to hear God's voice telling him that if he would listen, God would speak to him and give him guidance.

So at the next social gathering, he entered into the conversation and fun, but he kept his ears attuned to the Spirit. As he was talking and having a good time, he would sense the voice of the Spirit in his inner consciousness: "That's enough for now. Don't tell that next one." When he obeyed, he discovered that life was better. He went home feeling good about the evening instead of defeated.[16]

What would happen if we practiced God's presence in a similar way regarding all of life? In your sermon preparation, in your conversations, in your strategic planning, why not ask the Spirit to be your unseen, but not silent, partner? Listen for his voice. Respond to his gentle nudges. Would this not enable you to come closer to fulfilling God's potential for you and your ministry?

Fulfilling Your Potential

What is your potential? What size church can you lead? What types of ministry are you best suited to direct? How will you go about discovering your full potential?

Examine Your Style

What is your leadership style? How does it affect your potential? Peter Drucker put little stock in style. His observations led him to believe that leaders of various styles could be effective. You have probably known pastors who are people persons and who hated to spend time in the office, while others like nothing better than being secluded with their books.

> **Effective Leaders**
>
> Peter Drucker taught that effective leaders know four simple things:
>
> 1. A leader has followers.
> 2. A leader emphasizes results.
> 3. A leader provides a positive example.
> 4. A leader has a keen sense of responsibility.[17]

Some pastors are Mr. Nice Guy, while others are all business and won't tolerate any foolishness from their staff. Some pastors have warm personalities, while others appear more distant. Some pastors seem close to their families, while others seldom mention their spouses or children.

Drucker, reflecting on this apparent lack of coordination between style and effective leadership, said, "The one and only personality trait the effective ones I have encountered did have in common was something they did *not* have: they had little or no 'charisma' and little use either for the term or what it signifies."[18]

So don't be misled by too much emphasis on your style, as if to say, "If I don't have charisma or a certain leadership style, my potential will be limited." Leaders of all stripes manage to bring out enormous potential in themselves and others.

Experiment with Your Gifts

How has God gifted you? Do you have the gift of leadership? Service? Faith? Mercy? What comes easily to you? What do you really like to do? These are all keys to identifying your gifts, which will give you the greatest return for your investment of time and energy.

Do you know what your spiritual gifts are? If not, make it a priority to take a spiritual gifts inventory and discover how God has gifted you. You will be most effective when you are operating in an area that allows you to use your primary spiritual gifts.

Explore Your Fears

Has God placed some great project on your heart, some great enterprise that would glorify him and help people? Why have you hesitated in getting started in that project? Why have you not taken the first step?

Often the answer has to do with our fears. We are afraid we may fail. John M. Wilson observed, "Fear, if allowed free rein, would reduce all of us to trembling shadows of men, for whom only death could bring release."[19]

When you give in to your fears, you severely limit your potential. American industrialist Henry Ford said, "One of the greatest discoveries a man makes, one of his great surprises, is to find he can do what he was afraid he couldn't do."[20]

Extend Your Reach

What self-imposed boundaries could you push beyond this week? This month? This year? Someone did an experiment with a hungry barracuda and its natural food, a Spanish mackerel. They placed both fish in the same tank and slipped a glass partition down in the middle of the enclosure. The barracuda saw the mackerel and begin to swim toward it. Suddenly his nose smashed into the invisible glass and he stopped. He circled around and tried it again. Once again the transparent glass stopped him.

After the barracuda suffered several more nose-bashing experiences, the experimenters removed the glass. The hungry fish would only swim as far as where the glass had been. As long as the mackerel stayed on his own side of the tank, he was safe from the barracuda.

What nose-bashing experiences have stopped you from reaching beyond some invisible boundary? What do you need to do to exceed your current margins? Georges Clemenceau, the renowned French statesman, said, "A man's life is interesting primarily when he has failed—I well know. For it's a sign that he tried to surpass himself."[21]

Don't be afraid to try just because you have failed before. Your potential is waiting.

Your Potential

In his senior year as a tight end for the University of Minnesota Golden Gophers, Ben Utecht experienced a serious injury. As a result, the highly touted National Football League prospect faced the unwelcome prospect of not being drafted.

Before the draft, Indianapolis Colts coach Tony Dungy, who also had played for Minnesota, told Utecht, "Ben, I know you've just had this injury and if for some reason you don't get drafted, I promise you this: I will be the first person to call you." Two minutes after the draft began, Ben's phone rang.

Even though Ben couldn't play a single game in his first NFL season, the Colts paid him as if he were a starter. Three years later, he helped them win Super Bowl XLI.[22]

Coach Dungy hired an injured player because he believed in Ben Utecht's potential. Few of us could play in the NFL, but you have more potential than you realize. You can be the pastor God intended you to be. But before you begin packing, ask yourself: "Will this position challenge me to reach more of my potential, or am I better suited to stay where I am?"

Action Steps

1. List the kinds of assignments you have had. What do these experiences tell you about your God-given potential?
2. Discuss your ambitions with a friend. Does your friend agree or disagree with your assessment of your own potential? If he or she disagrees, what are the main points of disagreement?

4

VISION
Understanding the Need for Change

Changes in ministry will come whether we're ready or not. So prepare yourself for change.

Change happens. If we don't choose it, it chooses us.
—EDWARD GRINNAN

Motivational speaker Les Brown tells the story of a man walking down the street on his way to work. He observed there were dogs on almost every front porch and they would all bark as the man walked past them. One little dog, however, just sat there, whimpering, whining, and moaning, as if he were in pain.

Day after day, this was the scene he witnessed. While all the other dogs barked, this particular dog just whined and moaned. After a week or so, the man's curiosity got the best of him. He walked up to the house where the whimpering dog sat on the porch and knocked on the door.

The owner of the dog answered the door and the man asked, "Sir, is this your dog?" When the owner replied in the affirmative, the man asked, "Why does he sit here, moaning and groaning, whimpering and whining, while all the other dogs on this block are barking?"

"Well," said the owner, "he's actually sitting on a nail."

"What? If he's sitting on a nail, why doesn't he get off?"

"Well, I guess it just doesn't hurt him enough."[1]

As silly as that story is, I'm afraid I've known a pastor or two who remained in an extremely painful situation much longer than necessary. I can only imagine they just didn't hurt enough to make a change.

Sometimes we need a change. We are ready for a change. Conditions are ripe for a change. Some people seem to grasp this, understand it, and act upon it, while others seem to resist it, block it, deny it, and continue sitting on the nail far too long.

No Change, No Growth

Life is full of changes. They're unavoidable. The only way to achieve growth and maturity is through change. No change, no growth.

Change or Stagnation

In many new suburban subdivisions around the country, developers have built retaining ponds. They install fountains in these ponds that spray the water into the air, often creating a beautiful effect, especially if the area around the pond is well landscaped and neatly trimmed. The ponds are necessary to facilitate water drainage. But without movement, the picturesque water would become green with algae and would soon present an eyesore.

In life, as well as in retention ponds, no change leads to stagnation. No change means slow but certain death. You can change without growing, but you cannot grow without changing.

Midcourse Corrections

The late astronaut James Irwin said, "You might think going to the moon was the most scientific project ever, but they literally 'threw us' in the direction of the moon. We had to adjust our course every ten minutes and landed only inside fifty feet of the five-hundred-mile radius of our target."[2]

Those who are unwilling to make midcourse corrections are not likely to land where they want to be.

Seven Ways to Tell if You Need Change

Judith Sills, PhD, suggests seven ways to tell if you need change:

1. The counter boy at Dunkin' Donuts calls you by name.
2. Dust balls fly when you get out the exercise mat.
3. On Monday, you start wishing for Friday.
4. You lose patience with your children and your coworkers.
5. It's been two years since you tried a new cologne.
6. All you seem to do on Saturdays is run errands.
7. A sunset doesn't take your breath away.[3]

How to Tell if You Need a Change

How does a pastor know if he or she needs a change?

You may think a change is in order if you have had trouble getting others to change. Every pastor, even one with minimal experience, knows the difficulty in persuading others to accept change. It requires an act of God to change a person from a sinner to a saint. It may also nearly require an act of God to get regular attendees to move close to the front of an auditorium so latecomers can sit in the back, without the embarrassment of having to walk up front to find a seat.

Getting Others to Change

Pastors who experience one frustration after another in getting people to change may feel like Calvin of the *Calvin and Hobbes* comic strip. One comic strip portrays Calvin and his stuffed-tiger friend hurtling down a hill on their wagon. Calvin yells to Hobbes, "I thrive on change."

The surprised tiger yells back, "You? You threw a fit this morning because your mom put less jelly on your toast than yesterday."

Calvin explains, "I thrive on making other people change."[4]

Part of a pastor's job is getting people to change. But no one can force the issue. We use the power of persuasion to help people see the need for changing behavior and attitudes. One pastor confessed, "I came to the place where I felt I was beating my head against the wall. Why couldn't they see what I was trying to teach?" He was ready for a change.

Dean Hoge and Jacqueline Wenger allude to the dynamics of push and pull in ministry transition. There are forces that push us involuntarily toward transition, while other forces pull us voluntarily toward transition.[5] The voluntary pull may be the influence of the Holy Spirit. It may also be the natural growth of one's expertise, crying out for a greater challenge.

The involuntary forces that push us toward transition may include local leaders who are ready for a change, denominational executives who see the need for a change, or unforeseen circumstances that bring a crisis to a head and necessitate a change.

Change: Good or Bad?

Not all change is good. One pastor felt trapped in his routine and wanted something different. He felt he needed a change of pace. Although he was not ready to leave his church, he wanted a new challenge.

He decided to spend a week at a dude ranch in Texas. When he arrived, he admitted to the director that he did not know much about riding a horse but was eager to learn. The director smiled and said, "No problem. We have all kinds of horses for all kinds of people. For big people we have big horses. For small people we have small horses. For people who want to go fast, we have fast horses. For those who want to go slow, we have slow horses. For those who are experienced horsemen, we have experienced horses. And for those who have never ridden a horse, we have horses that have never been ridden!"

As I said, not all change is good.

When Conflict Leads to Change

Sollie grew up in a traditional religious family that took its heritage seriously. He followed in the footsteps of his ancestors who were conservative. He studied hard and became well versed in his religion. Joe was not so much an intellectual as he was a people person. Generous, with a warm smile and an encouraging word, Joe became one of Sollie's best friends. Maybe they got along well because they were so different from one another. As they say, opposites attract.

When they met, Sollie was in some trouble, having developed a reputation as a severe, zealous person, who was more interested in being right than in caring about people and their feelings. At the drop of a hat, he would debate anybody who challenged his faith. In spite of Sollie's abrasiveness, Joe liked him and saw his potential as a Christian worker. So he intervened with the church board, whose members were cautious about accepting Sollie.

In time, church leaders recognized Sollie's potential too. In fact, they chose Joe and Sollie to co-lead a short-term missions trip. Joe persuaded his cousin John to go along, so they shipped out and traveled from place to place, spreading God's Word and encouraging new Christians. They genuinely enjoyed the experience of working together in cross-cultural ministry. Sollie's boldness, even when faced with cases of demon possession and opposition from local leaders who resented their interference, was an inspiration. They saw many people come to Christ and the whole experience strengthened their resolve to work even harder for the Lord.

When they returned, they gave a glowing report of what the Lord had accomplished through their efforts. Their local church was thrilled.

Sometime later, they agreed they should take another short-term missions trip, so they began to make plans. It wasn't long, though, before they ran into a difference of opinion about who should go with them. It seems a shame, looking back, that two good friends should come to such sharp disagreement that they would have to part company. But their controversy led them to agree to disagree. It became a point of transition.

So Joe—Joseph Barnabas—took his cousin John Mark, and sailed for Cyprus, his home region, where he and Sollie had gone before. John Mark was the focus of the controversy. He had apparently deserted the fledgling missionary party on their first trip and returned to more comfortable surroundings. Sollie, Saul of Tarsus, did not trust John Mark and did not think it wise to take him with them again. Instead Saul departed for Cilicia, his home region, and took Silas as his missionary companion (see Acts 15:36–41).

It was time for a change. Neither Saul nor Barnabas sought the change. Neither wanted it. But contentious circumstances drove them in separate directions. In the long run, the separation was probably for the best. Instead of one missionary party, the young Christian church now had two stalwart missionaries, leading their protégés in adventures for Christ. They had twice as many workers strengthening new believers in foreign fields, as well as reaching more converts to Christianity.

Although Saul and Barnabas disagreed sharply, Saul's subsequent actions showed he had learned a great deal from Barnabas, who had earlier been his mentor. By dividing into two groups, they could "accomplish two goals: minister to the target group *and* train . . . associates as ministers."[6] They achieved evangelism and mentoring all at the same time.

The point of transition led to a principle that Saul (Paul) would later recommend to Timothy: "You then, my son, be strong in the grace that is in Christ Jesus. And the things you have heard me say in the presence of many witnesses entrust to reliable men who will also be qualified to teach others" (2 Tim. 2:1–2).

Not all change is good. But neither is all change bad.

The Stages toward Embracing Change

In 1803, the British created a new position, a civil service job requiring a man to stand on the cliffs of Dover with a spyglass. Authorities charged him with the responsibility to watch for an invasion by Napoleon Bonaparte. If he saw the French army approaching, he was to ring a bell.

That was an important job in 1803. However, no one got around to eliminating the job until 1945, when Napoleon had been dead for more than one hundred twenty years![7]

Familiarity unto Death

A naval aviator made the observation that many pilots have died because they stayed with their disabled aircraft too long. "They preferred the familiarity of the cockpit to the unfamiliarity of the parachute, even though the cockpit had become a death trap."

—Nido Qubein[8]

How many of us have been so focused on what we're doing that we are not even open to the idea of change? Too many of us have concentrated on the task at hand until we are unaware that the world is changing around us and we need to change too.

Most of us are slow to accept change. In the case of ministry, we don't want to give up; we want to persevere. So we may be reluctant to admit the need to change. Dennis O'Grady suggests five stages we typically go through before we embrace change.[9]

Crisis

Not every crisis signals a need for change. Many crises are opportunities for ministry. If tragedy such as a fire, tornado, or flood strikes a community, those are times for ministry. If parishioners go through the crisis of unemployment, death, or some other calamity, those are opportunities for ministry.

If it becomes a crisis of confidence, however, in which parishioners lose faith in their pastor even if the pastor is innocent of wrongdoing, it may be time for a change. A prominent family may leave the church, or a strong giver transfers to a different city. Depending on the strength of the church, this may signal a crisis. Dr. O'Grady identifies the sense of crisis as a wake-up call, telling us we must confront the need for a change.

Hard Work

You may perceive that you simply need to work harder. The answer to the crisis may be to take a class, read some pertinent books, or network with successful pastors. By engaging in the hard work of learning a new skill or of becoming immersed in continuing education, you retain a sense of control. You are working hard to figure out a solution to this crisis.

One pastor attended a leadership conference. He had tried without success to turn his church around. In spite of his best efforts, the church continued to decline. He hoped the conference would give him the added insights and skills that would turn the tide. He even managed to have breakfast with the conference leader, who advised him to go back home, apply the principles he had learned, but not to feel locked in forever. The leader suggested that, after a year or so, if things were not changing for the better, he could conscientiously look for another assignment. A year later, other opportunities did open up and he moved, feeling he had done his best before changing.

Tough Decision

Finally, you have to make a decision. By definition, tough decisions are not easy. But it does often provide relief just to get off the fence and make a decision. Standing at a fork in the road, considering two, three, or more options, can tie the stomach in knots and keep you awake at night. Charting a new course can set you free. It often brings a feeling of optimism.

Making a tough decision may be the first step toward improving yourself, which can be a giant step toward improving your own world.

Effective Leaders

Anne Frank said, "How wonderful it is that nobody need wait a single moment before starting to improve the world."[10]

Unexpected Pain

Unfortunately, sometimes we do the right thing but get the wrong results. That's when we're tempted to give up on our goals. Yet, as trite as it sounds, there's no gain without pain. We have to anticipate that even a good decision may run into some obstacles.

Lewis Smedes declares, "Pain is God's hammer and chisel—to sculpt out character and chip out vices."[11] Making a decision—even the right decision—may include pain. If you keep going in the right direction, you will eventually reach the next stage.

Joy and Integration

This is the stage at which you begin to see the wisdom of your choices. You look back and recognize the changes you made were for the better. They have paid off.

When you can see joy in adversity, you have passed the joy and integration stage.

When All Else Fails

But what if you are stuck in one of the stages and can't seem to figure out what to do next?

Be open to opportunities. Sometimes we encounter crossroads in life unexpectedly. And crossroads present us with options. Keep your eyes and ears open.

Joy in Adversity

Kurt Warner, quarterback of Super Bowl XXXIV champion St. Louis Rams, and his wife Brenda, have a child, Zachary, who was accidentally dropped at the age of four months. He is blind. The doctor had said his life wouldn't be very productive. Kurt and Brenda feel Zachary has taught them much about love and joy. Brenda said, "I want people to know that the same joy that we have now is the joy we had when my son was injured, the joy that we had when my parents were killed in a tornado. The joy is not circumstantial. It is from a deeper, bigger God than we all can even imagine."[13]

Be willing to change. Most of us resist change. But change is inevitable. If you learn to be adaptable and grow through change, you will be a happier person. As Edward Grinnan says, "Change happens. If we don't choose it, it chooses us."[12]

Be conscious of the need for a mentor. Maybe you know someone who seems comfortable with change. You have watched him or her embrace change, even though it may have been a difficult transition. Chances are that person will be glad to talk about it. Be willing to learn from that individual.

Be willing to give up control. Admit it: You can't control everything anyway. Author Dale Hanson Bourke says, "We have to offer up a clean slate of expectations and plans and let God control the outcome."[14]

Mastering Change

Dr. Sheila Murray Bethel reminds us that we live in an exciting age of unprecedented change. Because change is inevitable, we must learn to use it to best advantage. She suggests four ways to master change.[15]

Don't Fight It

One of the reasons we resist change is because we grow comfortable with the way things are. We want to protect what is familiar. People who try to form new habits soon realize the biggest obstacle is their love for the old habit.

Successful pastors soon learn, when they change churches, that they cannot lead the new church in exactly the same way as the old church. While human nature is much the same the world over, local personalities differ, local conditions fluctuate, and local problems may throw you a new curve that you have never before seen.

When you fight change, you only complicate your life. You contribute to your own stress and may even become ill. Don't fight it. Pray that God will give you the courage to change what you can and the grace to accept what you cannot change.

Escaping Old Ideas

"The real difficulty lies not in developing new ideas, but in escaping from the old ones."

—John Maynard Keynes[16]

You Don't Have to Like the Change

Some things about your new situation may almost drive you crazy. You may wonder, "Why in the world did I agree to this change? We were so happy in our previous church." First of all, be sure you have an inner assurance that the change is God's direction for you, as best you can tell. Then when the transition sets in and changes begin to accumulate, you can rest assured that God will never take you where his grace cannot keep you. You can remind yourself, to paraphrase Romans 5:20, "Where problems increase, grace increases all the more."

Meanwhile, arm yourself with greater knowledge. Get to know the people, familiarize yourself with the new community, and acquaint yourself with the new church's customs and traditions. All these things will enable you to better handle the change.

Know What to Defend against Change

Change only for the sake of change is seldom good. Know what the nonnegotiables are in your life. Know yourself. While you can change and adapt yourself to a new situation, you cannot change your basic personality and temperament—at least not without help from God.

It is wholesome to learn new skills and find ways to improve our performance. But know yourself well enough to resist getting into a situation that would require you to be a different type of person—unless you are willing to make major adjustments. Just as it's almost impossible to change other people against their will, you are probably not going to change who you are either, unless you are highly motivated.

Perhaps you heard about the derelict man standing on a street corner in the Wall Street district of New York City, begging for money. As a corporate executive passes by, the derelict reaches out his hand and pleads, "Change? Change?"

The corporate executive, already stressed, responds with a pained expression and says, "I'm trying! I'm trying!"[17]

It's like the old joke about how many psychologists it takes to change a lightbulb. Only one, of course, but the lightbulb really has to want to change! Know yourself, your gifts, and your family well enough that you know what to defend against change.

Have a Sense of Humor

As Dr. Bethel points out, a sense of humor can give you a "momentary emotional vacation."[18] You can plow through a lot of stuff in life if you're willing to see the humor in it. On the other hand, as the old saying goes, "If you take yourself too seriously, no one else will." The ability to laugh at yourself and the situation can get you through some very difficult times.

Gelantology

A 2005 University of Maryland School of Medicine study in the field of gelantology—the study of laughter—indicates laughter improves the function of blood vessels and is good for the heart.[19] Other researchers have shown that laughter boosts the immune system and reduces levels of stress hormones.[20]

Long before scientists used modern research methods, the Bible said, "A cheerful heart is good medicine" (Prov. 17:22). If you laugh at yourself and your situation, you will likely live longer.

Changing Yourself

Change is inevitable. But while you're thinking about changing parishes, don't forget to consider changing yourself. Unfortunately, as Russian writer Leo Tolstoy pointed out, "Everyone thinks of changing the world, but no one thinks of changing himself."[21]

An Anglican bishop, who lived around A.D. 1100, wrote the following words near the end of his life:

> When I was young and free and my imagination had no limits, I dreamed of changing the world. But as I grew older, I realized the world would not change. So I shortened my sight somewhat and decided to change only my country. But it too seemed immovable. As I grew into my twilight years, in one last desperate attempt, I settled for changing only my family, those closest to me. But alas, at that age, they would have none of it. Now as I lie on my death bed, I realize that if I had only changed myself first, then by example, perhaps I would have changed my family. From their inspiration and encouragement to me, I would have been better able to help my country and maybe even help change the world.[22]

When the time comes for you to make a change—whether you initiate it or others suggest it—when you're convinced it is inevitable, don't run from it; embrace it. Look forward to how God will bless you, change you, and work through you in a new way.

Action Steps

1. Reviewing the section on the stages of change, at what stage are you? What would it take to move to the next stage? What would it take to bring joy and integration?
2. Think through the nonnegotiables in your life. What things are you unwilling to change? Why?

5

Perseverance

Staying When You Have an Offer You Can't Refuse

To go or to stay: it's a debate in which you must engage when faced with an offer you can't refuse.

If you start something, finish it!
—Henry Ford

Pastor Michael's heart raced as he hung up the phone. The voice on the other end of the line had just offered him a job he had always wanted.

"We would like you to come and head the pastoral ministries department of our Christian university," the president had said.

For years, Michael had told his wife, "Someday, when I get tired of the pastoral routine and am ready for another challenge, I would like to teach young ministers-in-training."

The president had just handed him such an offer. Yes, there would be administrative duties involved, so it wouldn't be all teaching. Yet it would put him in the world of academia, right in the middle of young women's and men's lives at a crucial point just before they launched into lifelong ministries. It would be Michael's chance to influence the next generation of pastors, missionaries, and Christian workers.

On the other hand, he had only served his present church for three years. The church had experienced a 40 percent gain in worship attendance, added new members, and maintained great momentum. "How often does that happen?" he thought. "I have never experienced this level of growth and this depth of satisfaction with ministry in my previous twenty-five years of pastoral service. If I leave now, this church will likely suffer a stall in its momentum."

He had assembled an excellent staff, but he also knew they had not worked together for very long. He was not confident they would mesh gears for successful ministry if he disrupted the balance in leadership at this point.

What to do? Obviously, prayer would be the first thing to do. But, as excited as he was about the prospects, Michael knew he would have to weigh all the circumstances. And, of course, he wanted to discuss it with Judy, his wife, immediately.

It was an offer he could hardly refuse. Yet, was that a good enough reason not to persevere in his present assignment when things were going so well?

Persevering through Problems

Pastorates are temporary. As disappointing as that may sound, let's be honest: most are not lifelong assignments. Especially in the early years of ministry, a change of assignment may come every few years, until pastoral spouses begin to say, "I am not going to move one more time! We must stay put long enough for our kids to have some stability. And I get so tired of making friends, only to pull up roots and head for another church."

Of course, I have some pastor-friends who have led their churches for many years. But they are the exception, not the rule. Most of us know that another offer will come our way before too much time elapses. In fact, many hope another offer will come soon!

Especially if you happen to be in the midst of a conflict when that offer comes, it may seem like an "offer you can't refuse."

No pastor wants the reputation: "Well, he just doesn't seem to stay in place very long" or "She moves around a lot." We would prefer to have a reputation for perseverance, for having the ability to weather the storms, surmount the problems, and come out into the sunshine.

When faced with a tempting offer, prayer is the best way to find direction. No one can argue with the challenge to pray. Yet prayer does not rule out thinking through the situation, looking at the pros and cons, talking with trusted friends and mentors, and examining your own motives. But you could do all these things and remain uncertain as to what decision you should make.

> **Perseverance**
>
> "Problems of any sort raise key questions about perseverance. How can I know whether the troubles I currently suffer are a circumstantial sign from God that he has a new direction for me? How do I know if my circumstances are something God wants me to endure and then grow through?"
>
> —Craig Brian Larson[1]

No wonder the ancient wise man recommended, "Trust in the Lord with all your heart; do not depend on your own understanding. Seek his will in all you do, and he will show you which path to take" (Prov. 3:5–6 NLT).

Brian Ray suggests another strategy when standing at the crossroads, wondering whether to move ahead or to hold steady. He cites Jeremiah 6:16, in which the prophet advises, "This is what the LORD says: 'Stand at the crossroads and look; ask for the ancient paths, ask where the good way is, and walk in it, and you will find rest for your soul.'"

Ray focuses on the verbs in that verse: stand, look, ask, and walk. Before we walk through a crossroads, we need to stand still long enough to look carefully and ask the right questions.[2]

Crucial questions to ask when you're considering a pastoral transition include being brutally honest enough to say, "Is the job the problem or am I the problem?" Is my board behaving badly or am I behaving badly? Whatever your answers, thinking through the issues can be extremely helpful. If you're going to change, you want to be sure you're changing for the right reasons.

Furthermore, think about your primary gifts. Moving to another position, even if it looks like an offer you can't refuse, is not wise if you are getting too far away from the best use of your gifts. There's more at stake here than your job satisfaction. Dave Frakes observes, "My gifts are not for me; they are for other people. If I am not using them, I am not being a good steward of what God has given me."[3]

God already knows which way you're going to decide, of course, and nothing you do will catch him off guard. He is preparing your work in advance. That's exactly what Paul said: "For we are God's workmanship, created in Christ Jesus to do good works, which God prepared in advance for us to do" (Eph. 2:10).

So in facing the challenge of finding God's will for your future, you can whittle the offer down to size if you stop and look long enough to ask the right questions before you walk through the crossroads.

Persevering through the Distractions

If you do a good job, keep your nose clean, and achieve a reasonable amount of success, sooner or later you will receive an offer you can't refuse. In the strictest sense, there is no such thing as an offer you can't refuse. You always have a choice. The consequences of your choice may be disagreeable, but you always have a choice.

The temptation to leave where you are may come from those who are impressed with you or it may come from your detractors, those who do not appreciate your success.

That's what happened to Nehemiah, an official in the court of King Artaxerxes of Persia in the fifth century B.C. He and his fellow countrymen were transplanted Jews, descendants of those whom the Babylonians took captive and transported to Babylon over a twenty-year period from 606 to 586 B.C. When Persia conquered the Babylonians in 536, King Cyrus, a "singularly noble and just monarch,"[4] began to permit Jews to return to Jerusalem.

Nearly a hundred years later, however, the city and especially the wall were still in disrepair. When Nehemiah heard about the condition of Jerusalem, his heart ached to do something about it. The people of Jerusalem were in "great trouble and disgrace" because the wall of the city had been broken down and the gates burned (Neh. 1:3).

Nehemiah wept. He also prayed. Unable to conceal his dismay, Nehemiah's countenance attracted the king's attention.

When the king inquired as to the cause of his sadness, Nehemiah admitted it was because of Jerusalem's condition. The king asked him what he wanted, and Nehemiah seized the opportunity to request a leave of absence. He also asked for letters to provide safe conduct, and permission to take supplies for rebuilding the wall.

Once he was in Jerusalem, Nehemiah toured the city wall, noting its condition and making plans for its repair. He assembled the people, inspired them to do the work, and organized them for the project.

His neighbors soon interfered with the work. Sanballat, Tobiah, and Gesham began to mock and ridicule Nehemiah and the project. Whether their opposition came from politics, jealousy, or racial tensions (Sanballat, for instance, was a Samaritan, not considered a pure Jew), their hostility provided a distraction.

Nehemiah had already left a "plum job," in which he enjoyed the comforts of palace employment in Persia. The project in Jerusalem involved extensive hard labor. Now the appeal tempted him to go back where he came from and leave well enough alone.

I know pastors who have felt just this kind of opposition. Sometimes a transplant from one part of the country to another finds it difficult to identify with local customs and traditions. The local natives may become irritated and feel the pastor does not fit in.

If the pastor also happens to be a visionary and has the audacity to suggest we might not continue to do things the way we've always done them, detractors may show up to point out the advantages of leaving. Does the pastor yield to those temptations? After all, it may well be easier to leave and go where one is wanted than to stay and fight through the opposition.

If your call is firm and you cannot feel clear in your heart to leave, it's better to pray for internal strength and external reinforcements, and stay where God has called you.

What did Nehemiah do? It wasn't easy to feel the sting of Sanballat's sarcasm: "What are those feeble Jews doing? . . . Can they bring the stones back to life from those heaps of rubble—burned as they are?" (Neh. 4:2). It wasn't easy to hear Tobiah's taunts: "What they are building—if even a fox climbed up on it, he would break down their wall of stones!" (Neh. 4:3).

Nehemiah responded by praying to God with an imprecatory plea: "Hear us, O our God, for we are despised. Turn their insults back on their own heads. Give them over as plunder in a land of captivity. Do not cover up their guilt or blot out their sins from your sight, for they have thrown insults in the face of the builders" (Neh. 4:4–5).

Fortunately, Nehemiah's actions were nobler than his prayer. He simply went to work and "rebuilt the wall till all of it reached half its height, for the people worked with all their heart" (Neh. 4:6). Your people, working with all their heart, are a great incentive to stay where you are.

A pastor-friend received an enticing invitation from his denominational supervisor, who explained why my friend would be ideal for the assignment he had in mind. After praying about it, the pastor answered, "It sounds like a great opportunity, but it seems the people here are finally all working together, moving in the same direction. I'd like to stay here a little longer and see what we can accomplish." It's difficult for a pastor to leave a group of people who are working in unison, "working with all their heart."

When Nehemiah's detractors saw how successful he was, they tried one more distracting ploy: They offered to meet and talk. But Nehemiah saw through their schemes. He answered, "I am carrying on a great project and cannot go down. Why should the work stop while I leave it and go down to you?" (Neh. 6:3).

You can refuse an offer you can't refuse if you're sold on the job you have now, feel committed to it, sense the people's support, and most of all, feel God's thumb in your back to persevere and stay.

Lessons in Perseverance

Considering an offer you can't refuse can tempt you to throw in the towel before God is ready for you to quit.

Someone approached Francis of Assisi while he was hoeing his garden. "What would you do if you were suddenly told you'd die at sunset today?" the person asked. He responded, "I'd finish hoeing my garden."

George Sweeting, referring to that story, said, "Our perseverance doesn't change God—it changes *us*. If we're willing to continue—even when we feel like quitting—we'll learn lessons of compassion, understanding, and dependability."[6]

The Will to Persevere

"The will to persevere is often the difference between failure and success."

—David Sarnoff[5]

Compassion

In our generation, probably no one more consistently symbolizes the word *compassion* than Mother Teresa. She chose to devote her life to the ministry of caring for the homeless and dying of Calcutta. Together with her Missionaries of Charity she won approval from the authorities in Calcutta to use an abandoned Hindu temple as a home for the dying.

Hindu priests in the area became uncomfortable with a missionary organization setting up shop in their neighborhood so close to their existing temple. They petitioned city authorities to relocate the home for the dying.

Priests from the temple led a large delegation to demand that the missionaries leave. Mother Teresa came out and addressed the crowd. "If you want to kill me," she told them, "here I am! You can merrily behead me. But do not disturb my poor patients."

Sometime later she became aware that one of the Hindu priests was dying, the victim of an advanced stage of tuberculosis. His case was deemed untreatable, so the city hospital had denied him a bed. Mother Teresa brought the dying priest to her facility, where she personally cared for him until the day he died. Then the Missionaries of Charity took his body back to the temple so they could administer his last rites as a Hindu.

That act of compassion "captured the hearts of the people of Calcutta."[7] She earned their admiration because she persevered. When pastors reject the offer they can't refuse and stay with their congregations, they rise in the esteem of their people. Pastors often preach a high level of commitment to their people. When they place a priority on persevering with a local congregation, it shows their compassion is real, not fake. It also speaks volumes about their loyalty or their dependability.

Loyalty

Stuart Briscoe observed the behavior of salesmen who seemed enthusiastic about their products. They gave convincing presentations. Yet a few months later, he was amazed to find them working for their former competitors. When he inquired about their abandonment of the products they claimed were superior in favor of products they had previously declared inferior, he "discovered their commitment was more to their percentage than their product."[8]

The pastor's loyalty must be to the people and the parish, not just to the paycheck. Pastors find their own loyalty often breeds loyalty on behalf of their laypeople. The pastor may at times feel like Billy Martin, the often-fired baseball manager. He once described a successful baseball coach as "the one who keeps the five players who hate him away from the four who are still uncertain."[9]

Most pastors will discover that loyalty breeds loyalty. If you are dependable, you can't guarantee everyone will follow your example. But if you are not dependable, you can be doubly sure that many will imitate your poor example. Persevering, when you could leave for another attractive assignment, speaks volumes to your congregation about your loyalty.

Ingrates

"When I make an appointment to a high office from among ten candidates, I make nine enemies and one ingrate."

—Abraham Lincoln[10]

I love the story of Elizabeth, the Queen Mother of England, and her attitude during the Blitz on London in 1940. Someone asked her whether the little princesses, Elizabeth and Margaret Rose, would leave England for their safety. The queen replied, "The children will not leave unless I do. I shall not leave unless their father does, and the king will not leave the country in any circumstances whatever."[11]

Blessed is the pastor who will not leave unless the King calls him or her to do so.

Understanding

Nearly every pastor has dealt with the disappointment of seeing valued members move away because of job changes. One can hardly blame breadwinners who take advantage of an offer that will improve their ability to provide for their family. I heard about a church planter in the Midwest who had accumulated a group of several families who were going to help him launch a new church. Within two months, all but one of those families transferred out of state for better-paying jobs.

So when laypersons see their pastor refuse an attractive offer and choose to stay with the church, it speaks volumes about loyalty, compassion, and understanding.

An anonymous thinker has determined key ingredients to understanding others:

- The least important word: *I.*
- The most important word: *We.*
- The two most important words: *Thank you.*
- The three most important words: *All is forgiven.*
- The four most important words: *What is your opinion?*
- The five most important words: *You did a good job.*
- The six most important words: *I want to understand you better.*[12]

Pastors who persevere and communicate that level of understanding will attract and retain loyalty from their people.

Persevering though Perplexed

My friend Ron told me he left a growing church and accepted a pastorate nine hundred miles distant only to face a crisis a few months later. The "new" church caught on fire when a ballast in a basement ceiling fluorescent light fixture malfunctioned. He wanted to "get the church on fire," but that was not his chosen method.

Before the fire department could extinguish the blaze, it caused considerable smoke damage in the church offices. He and his staff had to set up shop in the youth department. Instead of sitting at his lovely walnut desk, he used an eight-foot folding table and a metal folding chair. Not ideal for premarital counseling and a host of other necessary duties.

The phone company did install temporary phones, but three months is a long time to be displaced from familiar surroundings, interrupted by quick forays into the smoke-saturated interior of his office to grab a book or two.

In the midst of this displacement, his former denominational supervisor called. It seems his successor had a nervous breakdown and left Ron's previous church after a tenure of only five months. Would Ron be interested in returning? Shocked that he would even ask him to consider such a move after so short a time in his new post, Ron heard the official rationalize that sometimes moves did not turn out as well as intended and perhaps he had second thoughts about leaving.

Actually, he did have second thoughts about the transition. But ethically he could not justify leaving a pastorate in which he had invested so little, although the temptation was great to return to familiar surroundings, to an office not pungent with stale smoke, to people who loved him, and to a place where he felt comfortable.

As Ron discovered, there are several reasons to stay where you are instead of accepting an attractive option.

Avoid Second-Guessing Your Decisions

One of the easiest things in the world is to second-guess yourself. We can all get sidetracked thinking about the coulda/woulda/shouldas of life. It's always true that if we hadn't made one decision, we might have made another. And who knows how that would have turned out? You can play that game all day and wear yourself out, wondering what might have been.

Instead, put the past in the past and move on. Don't rehash your decisions. Live with the ones you've made.

No More Yesterdays

"Hourglass sand won't flow upward. The second hand of the clock refuses to tick backward. The monthly calendar reads left to right, not right to left. You no longer have yesterday."

—Max Lucado[13]

Realize Problems May Not Indicate God's Disfavor

Look at Joseph. Consider Job. Think of Jesus. They all underwent extreme suffering and deprivation. Yet they were all men who walked with God, who put God first in their lives. In large part, they suffered *because* they loved God and gave him priority.

C. S. Lewis pointed out that "Christians live in enemy territory and are engaged in guerrilla warfare against Satan."[14] If you're going through adversity, it's no sign God is unhappy with you. It may mean Satan is attacking you. It may mean you are simply experiencing what all people go through—the storms of life. Or you may have real human enemies. Whatever the cause, the answer is fight, not flight. When it's time to go, let it not be because you ran from a problem, but because you sensed God's direction in propelling you forward.

Understand Success May Not Indicate God's Blessing

We have to be smarter than that. You can probably think of examples of people who seemed to be at the top of their game only to discover they were really at the bottom of their character. In the 1980s, some television evangelists gave all of Christendom a black eye because their sins came to light at the height of their careers.

Some people achieve notable things because they are especially skilled, adept at using their gifts and talents to make money, or to achieve popularity, or to multiply friends, not necessarily because God is blessing them. If you're going through a valley, keep doing the right things and keep faith with God. Don't panic and run if a great offer comes along at the depth of a valley. Emotional and spiritual low points are seldom good places from which to make major decisions.

Recognize Adversity Is Not a Good Reason to Bail Out

Bad stuff happens to everybody. You may be going through some rotten things right now, but bailing out will not necessarily make it go away. You may change addresses, but that stuff has a way of stalking you, tracking you down, and nagging you with the memories of what might have been. If you stay and see it through, then when it does come time to leave, you can go with a clear conscience and a light heart.

Bobb Biehl asked a question during a time of economic downturn, but his question can apply to other types of adversity. "In this type of environment do I personally focus more on goals to be reached, problems to be solved, or opportunities to be seized?"[15] Many would have to admit it's none of the above, but rather they're focusing on the adversity itself. Not a productive option.

Believe Working through Difficulty Builds Character

The big question we often have to face is not "What are you going through?" but rather "What's going through you?" What are you processing and how are you processing it? What's happening in you is more important than what's happening to you.

Jim Collins cited research studies done by the International Committee for the Study of Victimization. These studies examined what happened to people who experienced serious adversity—things like battling cancer, suffering from accidents, being prisoners of war—and survived. They found people fell generally into three categories: "those who were permanently dispirited by the event, those who got their life back to normal, and those who used the experience as a defining event that made them stronger."[16] In which category do you generally find yourself?

Restaurateur Wolfgang Puck admitted, "I learned more from the one restaurant that didn't work than from all the ones that were successes."[17]

If adversity strengthens us, we could all profit from occasional problems. But don't go looking for them; they will find you.

Perspective on Perseverance

Pastor Michael mulled over the decision whether to leave his growing church to take his dream job, teaching and administering in a Bible college, with the opportunity to influence young women and men entering the ministry. He prayed about it, talked it over with his wife, and finally decided to stay where he was.

The Helpful Antagonist

"Our antagonist is our helper. He that wrestles with us, strengthens our muscles, and sharpens our skills."

—Edmund Burke[18]

Would he ever receive another opportunity to do what he had always wanted to do? He didn't know, and presumably neither did anyone else. But he had an inner affirmation that his decision was correct, that it was the right thing for now. All we can do is make the best decision possible, considering all the factors at hand. Ultimately Michael has to live with himself, his wife, and his God. His wife would have cooperated with whatever decision Michael made. But he decided to persevere rather than accept the offer he couldn't refuse.

More than ten years later, Pastor Michael (not his real name) has the luxury of perspective. In the three years that followed his decision, his church continued to grow, completed a successful building program, and added new ministries and staff. When Michael left to work as a denominational leader, his successor led the church into a growth phase that doubled previous attendance. Michael is glad for the growth he had, for the foundation he laid, and for the decisions he made.

Action Steps

1. Think through the possible repercussions of leaving your present parish. Is it worth it?
2. Make a list of the advantages and disadvantages of going and staying. Which outweighs the other? What does your gut tell you?

6

SUCCESSION
Preparing for the One Who Follows You

Like John the Baptist, you must decrease and your successor must increase.

The day I took this office, I began to prepare the way for my successor.
—DONALD SIEBERT, CEO OF J. C. PENNEY CO.

Astronaut James Lovell, along with several others, did what no other human beings have done before or since. They flew to the moon and either circled it or stepped foot on its surface. These astronauts form a league of extraordinary men whose deeds, at this writing, have not been replicated for more than thirty-six years.

Lovell and Jeffrey Kluger coauthored the book *Apollo 13*, which later became the basis for a popular motion picture. In a *Time* magazine article, Kluger tells about a conversation he had with Lovell regarding the fame resulting from the book and the motion picture. Lovell knew the notoriety would not last long.

He told Kruger, "Remember where you're standing when the spotlight goes off; you'll need to find your own way off the stage."[1]

Every pastor needs to hear that advice. Eventually, the spotlight goes out on your current ministry, and when it comes back on, it will be shining on someone else. Most pastors fade away quietly and move on to another parish, where a new spotlight awaits them. Occasionally, a pastor has trouble letting go and leaving the spotlight of the previous church. Frequent contacts with his former parish can make life merely irritable or nearly impossible for his successor.

The Leader Who Needed No Successor

Only one leader never needed a successor. Martin Luther believed, "There is one Leader who holds office in perpetuity, for whom no replacement is needed. It is a striking fact that His disciples make no move to appoint one of their number to take His place after His ascension, tacit evidence that they were gloriously conscious that He was still their living Leader. The church at times has lost the vivid sense of His presence, but there has never been the panic cry of a leaderless army. He has always demonstrated that the distresses and perils of His church lie deeply on His heart."[2]

You and Your Successor

No pastorate lasts forever. Whether your tenure is two years or twenty years, whether it ends in an orderly transition or a forced change, whether you resign or die in the pulpit, your successor will take over someday. He or she will sit in your desk chair, occupy your office, and preach in your pulpit. Ready or not, you will hand it all over to somebody else. So we may as well think in terms of preparing for a successor.

Some pastors have the opportunity to groom a successor. They bring on board a staff person who has the gifts and graces to become a senior pastor. The person stays long enough to gain sufficient credibility with the congregation to be accepted in that role. The senior pastor is able to pour himself into a successor so the life of the church continues with a seamless transition.

Stuart Briscoe of Elmbrook Church in suburban Milwaukee and Bob Russell of Southeast Christian Church in Louisville are notable examples of pastors who mentored their successors. In both cases, they brought onto their staffs younger men who later proved to have the leadership qualities essential for leading a great church.

For many others, the move to another parish comes too quickly to groom a successor. Or their church polity does not allow for this opportunity. A colleague in his first pastorate had led his church through a major building campaign, which added a new sanctuary and several classrooms. However, when it came to maintaining the parsonage, the board was too shortsighted to provide adequate closet space for the pastor and his family.

The pastor determined it would be unwise to press the issue with his board, so he called his district superintendent and said, "You are my superior; I would appreciate you going to bat for me on this issue." The pastor had discussed this issue with his superintendent a few weeks earlier, so the executive was surprised he didn't already have his closets. The relatively minor addition to the parsonage bedrooms would have cost a small fraction of what the church building program had cost.

A few days later, the superintendent called back to say, "I got your closets for you. You will be moving in June!"

No time to groom a successor. In reality, most pastors submit their resignation and stay out of the selection process for their replacement. You may have some very definite ideas as to the person who should replace you. You may think you know the kind of person who should be your successor. You may have a list of ideal qualities for the next pastor of your church. But you're better off to keep your ideas to yourself, even if asked, unless your denominational executive discusses it with you. As in most enterprises, you may be "too close to the forest to see the trees," and your opinions are justifiably biased.

A departing pastor is wise to focus not directly on his successor, but rather on the impact his leaving has on the people around him.

Impact on Family

The pastor's leaving will directly affect the parsonage family. His or her spouse and school-age children will feel the impact deeply. Family members may think, "Why is it that my spouse [parent] feels the call of God to go somewhere else and I have nothing to say about it?"

A pastor may be wise to consult family members and involve them in a discussion, even though he or she makes the final decision. I know several colleagues who, concerned about the impact of an impending move on their children, discovered that the children have a positive attitude. Having been reared in a home where they have heard their parents talk about the importance of obedience to God's will, they are not surprised when their parents choose to obey the Lord.

> **Quick to Obey**
>
> "Once we know God's will and timing, we should be instant to obey, taking action without delay. . . . The longer we take to act on whatever God wants us to do, the more unclear His directives become. We need to make sure that we are on God's interstate highway and not in a cul-de-sac."
>
> —John Mason[3]

Donald Bubna tells about one of his grandsons who was having a conversation with Bubna's daughter about missing

Grandma and Grandpa after they moved to a different church far from where the little boy lived. His mother affirmed that they did indeed miss them. The four-year-old paused and said, "Yes, but it's good that they obeyed God."[4]

Impact on Staff

Pastors who have staff persons working with them will want to be considerate of the impact the move will make upon these colleagues. Even in a solo ministry, the pastor will want to discuss the move with the governing board before announcing it to the congregation.

In some denominations, staff members are required to resign when the senior pastor resigns. So the lead pastor's decision has huge ramifications for those whose livelihood depends on their connection to the chief executive. The pastor is wise to discuss the impending move with staff persons before announcing it to the congregation.

Sensitivity to their needs during the transition process will be important. If they must resign, a generous and positive letter of reference from you may help them find new employment elsewhere.

Impact on the Congregation

Naturally, the pastor's leaving creates a huge impact on the congregation. Most will be sad that you are leaving. A few may be genuinely glad, in spite of their glowing words to the contrary. Your attitude about the move will be the single greatest factor in determining how they accept the change.

If you talk about it in terms of obedience to God's will, accepting his direction for your future ministry, they are likely to accept it well. If you're positive, they're likely to be positive. In the case of a forced move, your attitude is even more important. Taking the high road, refusing to criticize detractors, never showing a bad attitude, and speaking in positive terms of what God has next both for you and for the congregation will go a long way toward preventing any polarization of the church body.

Increasing and Decreasing

We find the classic example of preparing the way for one's successor in the New Testament. The air fairly crackled with excitement when, after a silence of four hundred years, God spoke to Israel through a prophet named John the Baptist. Seven hundred years earlier, Isaiah had said, concerning John, "He is a voice shouting in the wilderness, 'Prepare the way for the Lord's coming! Clear the road for him!'" (Matt. 3:3 NLT).

Beginning with the End in Mind

John began his ministry preaching repentance and talking about his successor: "He who comes after me has surpassed me because he was before me" (John 1:15). True, he was speaking about the Son of God, who existed in eternity before John was born. But how affirming if you

No Replacement

When Benjamin Franklin completed his service as minister to France and returned to the United States in 1785, Thomas Jefferson assumed the position Franklin had vacated. Receiving Jefferson's credentials, the French prime minister said, "Monsieur Jefferson, have you come to replace Dr. Franklin?"

Jefferson replied, "No, Your Excellency. No one could ever replace Dr. Franklin. I am only succeeding him."[5] What a great attitude toward one's predecessor.

No Place for Jealousy

Jealousy has no place in the heart of a pastor toward his or her successor. Marvin Olasky tells the story of Abraham Lincoln's wife, Mary Todd Lincoln, who seems to have snapped after the death of Willie, her favorite son. President and Mrs. Lincoln encountered General and Mrs. U. S. Grant, along with General and Mrs. Edward Ord. After making unkind remarks to Mrs. Ord, Mary Lincoln turned to Mrs. Grant and said, "I suppose you think you'll get to the White House yourself, don't you?"

Lincoln tried to intervene and his wife turned on him. According to one observer, the President "bore it as Christ might have done, with an expression of pain and sadness that cut one to the heart, but with supreme calmness and dignity."[6]

can speak positive words about the person who follows you in the pulpit of your church.

In a later testimony, when some of John's disciples asked him about the ministry of Jesus, who was beginning to attract many followers, John replied, "He must become greater and greater, and I must become less and less" (John 3:30 NLT). In a very real sense, that's what happens when your successor follows you: he or she becomes greater in the eyes of your parishioners and you become less and less.

This is not because your parishioners think less of you. They still revere you, love you, and appreciate your ministry. But the spotlight has moved. Your successor becomes brighter and brighter, while you step into the shadows.

Putting Aside Jealousy

The further test of John's commitment and character occurred when some of his disciples followed Jesus. When they asked Jesus where he was staying, he told them, "Come, . . . and you will see" (John 1:39). We observe no indication of jealousy on John's part, no attempt to prevent his disciples from leaving him and following Jesus.

Instead John accepted the inevitable. He practiced what he later declared and allowed Jesus to increase in the minds and hearts of his disciples, while he decreased.

John prepared the way for his successor by speaking positively about Jesus, by understanding their respective roles, and by pointing his disciples in the direction of our Lord. These are all things you can do for your successor too.

Grooming a Successor

Hundreds of years earlier, Joshua succeeded Moses. Their situation was different from John and Jesus in that Moses mentored Joshua for forty years. The older man brought the younger man alongside him. He allowed Joshua to watch him minister and to accompany him in ministry opportunities. When the spies entered the Promised Land, only Joshua and Caleb returned with a positive report, a sign of Joshua's character and leadership. When the people expressed hesitation, Joshua and Caleb advised them not to be afraid but to push ahead and take the land without fear (Num. 14:6–9).

When Moses commissioned Joshua as the next undershepherd to lead Israel, God affirmed Joshua as one in whom his Spirit dwelled (Num. 27:18). The people understood that Joshua, their God-anointed leader, was "filled with the spirit of wisdom because Moses had laid his hands on him" (Deut. 34:9).

When Moses died and Joshua assumed full leadership of Israel, he called the leaders of the people together and gave them instructions concerning the crossing of the Jordan River. They answered Joshua, "Whatever you have commanded us we will do, and wherever you send us we will go. Just as we fully obeyed

Moses, so we will obey you. Only may the LORD your God be with you as he was with Moses" (Josh. 1:16–17). The transition was seamless and uneventful at least in part because of the way Moses blessed his successor in the eyes of the people.

Blessing Your Successor

Elisha's succession of Elijah brought another dimension to the process. In this case Elisha, who had some kind of premonition that Elijah was about to depart, sought the older prophet's blessing. "Let me inherit a double portion of your spirit," he said (2 Kings 2:9). Or to say it another way, "Please let me . . . become your successor" (NLT).

Elisha's mentor "left it to God to confirm or deny the bequeathal"[7] when he said, "If you see me when I am taken from you, then you will get your request. But if not, then you won't" (2 Kings 2:10 NLT).

In truth, only God can confirm or deny the success of our successor, yet we can affirm the choice of the congregation or our superiors. We can speak in positive terms about the future of the church.

Taking Your Successor Seriously

The mainstream media has mentioned people like Rick Warren, pastor of Saddleback Church in Lake Forest, California, as a successor to Billy Graham—not in the sense of leading the Billy Graham Evangelistic Association (BGEA), but rather in terms of leadership in the broader evangelical church.

Warren, tired of comparisons between his ministry and Graham's, says, "I have said many times, there is no successor to Billy Graham. Who was Luther's successor? Who was Wesley's successor? God uses individuals in individual ways."[8]

While it is true that such outstanding personalities are difficult to follow, Billy Graham does have a successor in the person of his son Franklin, at least in the BGEA. When other powerful leaders pass from the scene, someone must pick up the torch and lead. In many parachurch organizations, board members are faced with the daunting task of finding a successor who can still garner support, both in prayer and in finances, similar to what the founder attracted.

Peaceful Transitions

In the political realm, countries and parties face the necessity of choosing successors who will place the state or organization in the best position to wield power and exert influence. Such transitions can be difficult and are not always peaceful.

King Charles II of Spain died in 1701. In spite of multiple marriages, he had been unable to produce an heir. Shortly after Charles' death, Philip V, the duke of Anjou, was confirmed as King of Spain. The lineage of Spanish royalty was intertwined with other royal families of Europe. Philip was also the grandson of King Louis XIV of France. This connection upset the balance of power among European states, and some thought it gave France a distinct advantage. Soon the various countries drew lines of loyalty, resulting in the Grand Alliance—with England, the Netherlands, Denmark, Austria, and Portugal on one side and France, Spain, and a number of small German and

Italian principalities on the other. The War of Spanish Succession lasted thirteen years, ending in 1714.[9]

Fortunately most pastoral transitions do not result in all-out war, and most do not even involve major hostilities. But unless Jesus returns first, you will have a successor.

Donald Siebert, in the quote at the beginning of this chapter, shows that he understood the company did not belong to him and that his tenure would be one chapter in the ongoing story of that organization.

Term Limits

In a similar way, pastors may begin to prepare for a successor long before they announce their resignation. Without being melodramatic about the fact that you will leave someday, you can talk about your vision for the church during the time God allows you to be their pastor. This subtly communicates that we do live with time limits, that none of us is indispensable, that God's plan for the church is bigger than any of our plans and will outlast our tenures.

After you have announced your resignation, you can speak even more emphatically about your successor. Just as the congregation has treated you and your family well, you are confident they will take care of the next pastor in a similar way. You can express confidence that God has prepared just the right leader to follow you and lead the church into its next chapter of ministry.

Separating Yourself

You can also help your successor immensely by making it clear to the congregation that you will no longer be their pastor. Although the new pastor will be different from you, with his or her unique gifts, ideas, and emphases, the new pastor will be God's person to lead the church after you're gone.

You can also emphasize the fact that you will separate yourself from the church and community for a season, possibly a lengthy season. Your move may take you far away so that frequent return visits are not practical. Or you may move only a few miles or stay within the same judicatory so that contacts with former members of the church are unavoidable. By making it clear upfront that you intend to leave and no longer be available for counseling, weddings, and funerals, you send a signal that the congregation must learn to love and trust its new pastor.

In all cases, be sure you leave an up-to-date list of members and attendees of the church, including as much contact information as you can. In these days of GPS, online maps, and direction finders, you may not think it necessary to leave directions. But a colleague who moved to a small-town church discovered several of his parishioners had rural addresses. While RR 2, Box 123 served the postman very well, it did not help the pastor at all in finding his sheep. He asked those who lived in rural areas for specific directions to their homes, in case he was needed, and nearly all complied with his request. Again, with GPS and online maps, perhaps this is not as important as it once was. But those electronic conveniences are not foolproof either, so leaving directions to homes in remote areas could be a real service of love to your successor.

Sowing the Seeds of Preparation

A Chinese emperor devised an ingenious way to choose a successor. He handed out seeds for people to grow. A boy named Ping took a seed, planted it, and nurtured it. Normally he had a green thumb and experienced great success in growing things. This time, though, he could not get the seed to grow.

On the appointed day, Ping took his empty pot to the designated place for the king to review. He observed others bringing beautiful flowers and young plants. When the king came to him, Ping told how he normally had success in growing things but could not make this seed grow. The king listened with interest, and then turned to the others. "Where you got your seeds from, I do not know," he said. "For the seeds I gave you had all been cooked."[10]

Unfortunately, no perfect seeds exist, cooked or otherwise, for choosing your successor. However, there are some things you can do to prepare the way for your successor to have a better beginning to his or her ministry after you've gone.

Being Optimistic

If you know the person who will succeed you, and you can honestly say positive things about your successor, you will help the cause greatly if you do so. You can speak optimistically about your confidence in his or her leadership of the church in the future. If you cannot honestly say anything complimentary, don't say anything at all.

You can encourage your people to close ranks behind their new leader and work hard to grow the church under the direction of their new shepherd.

Then leave. Go to your new assignment and trust God to take care of your former flock.

A Lengthy Separation

A lengthy separation from your former church is best. Hopefully, you will have opportunities to visit in the future. But visiting too soon is not wise. It stirs up old memories. Even if they are good ones, it draws attention away from the new pastor. After time, a return visit will be appropriate. If you return to the community without an invitation from the new pastor, and you intend to visit the worship service, always let the new pastor know you're coming. You may not be invited to participate, but it is a professional courtesy to let him or her know you're in the vicinity.

The Golden Rule

"Get out of the way of your successor and try and be an encouragement. . . . Treat him the way you want your predecessor to treat you when you arrive at your new field."

—Warren Wiersbe[11]

Sometimes when pastors leave a community, their married children will remain. This means the pastor will return to that city with some frequency. Grandchildren exert tremendous influence! If you return soon, you may want to avoid attending the service. No rule of thumb is perfect, but the golden rule applies: Treat your successor the way you would want him or her to treat you if the roles were reversed.

It's one thing to tell your parishioners in advance that you will not be available for weddings and funerals, but when they call you after a dear friend of yours has died, it's much more difficult to say no. Yet you must remember how crucial it is for the new pastor to bond with the parishioners, and a time of grief is one of the prime ways this happens for many people. If you get involved, it may short-circuit that process.

Cautions about Returning

If you find yourself in a position where you feel you must accept an invitation to return for some event, be sure you clear it with the new pastor. Most pastors are willing to involve a former pastor in the service in some way. But by getting his or her permission, you acknowledge the new pastor's authority and responsibility in the situation. By showing deference to the new leader, you help to establish the individual's credibility.

If you are invited to participate in a church anniversary or some other special event, and it seems appropriate to return, look for things to compliment that will reflect well on the new pastor's leadership. Perhaps there are a number of new people in the congregation; you can allude to this and compliment the growth. If the church has made physical improvements to the buildings or property, you can refer to this.

When you leave, leave. "Cleave unto your new flock," to paraphrase the biblical statement about a man leaving his parents and cleaving to his wife (Gen. 2:24 KJV).

Leaving the Spotlight

A. W. Tozer pastored for many years in Chicago, but he spent his later years in Toronto, Canada. Once he said that "leaving a church is like dying and going to heaven and looking back to see what kind of a fool your wife married."

Donald Bubna, citing that quotation, declares the real question "is not whether my wife's new husband is better than I. Rather, the question is, How have I prepared my wife for life without me? And now that I'm gone, can I trust God to provide for her?"[12]

The spotlight will dim; you will exit and graciously turn your flock over to a new shepherd. If you are healthy, you will move on to your new parish, where the spotlight will illuminate a whole new chapter in your ministry. If you are unhealthy, you may be tempted to cling to relationships in your former parish and make life miserable for your successor. We call such an unhealthy attachment *codependency*. Don't fall into that trap. Instead, enjoy the new spotlight of ministry, pour yourself into the work at hand, and entrust your former parish into the hands of God and your successor.

Action Steps

1. What are some things you hope your predecessor is doing to prepare for your coming to a new parish? In what similar ways are you preparing for your successor?
2. What persons or groups do you need to inform that you are leaving prior to your announcement to the congregation? How will you go about letting them know?

7

PREPARATION

Getting Ready for Your Next Ministry Assignment

The better prepared you are for your next church, the better your chances of success.

I cannot recall, in any of my reading, a single instance of a prophet who applied for the job.
—A. W. TOZER

It was Pastor Stephen's first board meeting, and not a regularly scheduled one at that. The trustees had requested a quick meeting after the service. As it turned out, all the board members were present and all could stay only for a few minutes.

Once they assembled around the tables in the boardroom, Pastor Stephen called the meeting to order and asked the head trustee to make his presentation. Gary said, "Well, as you know, we've wanted to replace the van, and Fred here has found one on the lot at Driscoll's Used Cars. It's a fifteen-passenger vehicle, relatively low mileage, good body integrity—no rust—and it's priced right. It seems ideal for our purpose, which is mainly to pick up kids for the midweek program."

After a few minutes of discussion, Fred made a motion to buy the van, Gary seconded it, and before Pastor Stephen could catch his breath, the board members all said, "Aye." A few stood as if to leave.

"Just a second," the pastor said. "How are we going to pay for it?"

The treasurer smiled at the pastor and said, "Oh, we'll pay for it from our reserves."

With that the group stood and began to chat with one another, leaving Pastor Stephen's head spinning. Fortunately, he had the presence of mind to catch himself before his jaw dropped.

He was truly in a new place with a new way of doing things.

Such a decision in his previous parish would have taken at least an hour's discussion, and it would have included a good deal of wrangling about whether the church could afford it and how on earth would they pay for it, with money so tight.

He had just moved five hundred miles from the old parish, where unemployment had struck several families in the church, including two of his board members. The new parish was more prosperous, with several entrepreneurs in the congregation, including some on the board.

Although Stephen was greatly relieved not to sit through another tense board meeting, he almost felt guilty for enjoying the relative ease with which the decision had been made. He was not totally prepared for life in this new parish, but just maybe he could get used to it.

Clarifying Expectations

A few years passed, and the church hosted a denominational executive from a distant state for a series of services. The guest speaker was also an adjunct professor at a nearby Bible college.

> **Adaptation**
>
> Famous leaders in church history have learned to adapt. Martin Luther "adapted the secular tunes sung in the bars and taverns of his day by writing Christian lyrics to them. John Wesley followed this path when he began speaking the gospel directly to the blue collar workers of England and gathered them into small groups that met in homes rather than cathedrals."
>
> —Gary L. McIntosh[1]

In private conversation, he asked Pastor Stephen, "How is this church different from your last one?"

Stephen told him the above story as an example of the difference, then said, "I soon found I could not lead this church the same way I led the last one, nor the one before that. Each church is unique, and I have had to change my leadership style to fit each situation."

"I wish every student at the Bible college could hear that," the professor replied. "In fact, with your permission I would like to share it with my students as an example of how we must adapt our ministry styles instead of expecting each church to adjust to the pastor. In reality, there's adjustment on both sides as the congregation discovers our strengths and shortcomings, and as we learn what makes them unique."

What Does the Church Expect of You?

Pastors can stumble over a number of pitfalls if they haven't done their homework about the next parish. For instance, if it is a small church and you are the only paid staff, who will clean the church? Who will mow the church lawn? Many people assume that since the pastor is already getting paid, why shouldn't he or she take care of the maintenance of the physical church plant?

One pastor told the story of moving into a new community. After a week or ten days, he called his board together. "I notice the grass is getting pretty tall on the church lawn, and it really needs to be mowed."

One deacon answered, "Our former pastor always mowed the lawn."

"Yes, I know," replied the pastor, "but I talked with him, and he doesn't want to do it anymore."

Better to clarify those matters up front if you have any inkling that parishioners may be expecting you to do it.

In fact, it's good to clarify expectations in as many areas as possible, so both you and the church have a clear idea of what to anticipate.

What Does the Church Expect of Your Family?

Does the church expect your family to take an active role? Many churches used to assume the pastor's wife would play the piano. As more pastors' wives have worked outside the home and have lessened their active church involvement, this expectation has changed in many places.

If the former pastor's spouse had a visible ministry in the church—played an instrument, directed the worship team, or led the women's (or men's) ministry—and especially if it was a positive experience, the church may, consciously or unconsciously, expect the new pastor's spouse to do the same.

If it was a bad experience (the spouse was domineering, demanding, or disappointing), the church board may want to limit the activities of the spouse. Either way, it is important for you to know. Fair or not, your family may be judged by the level of their involvement in the church, especially if previous pastors' families have set a pattern. While it is true that the church is hiring you, not your spouse, it will be good for you to know their expectations.

A colleague interviewed for a position as a denominational executive, overseeing pastors and churches. He asked what the expectations were for his wife. The search committee indicated they simply wanted the spouse to use her gifts in whatever way she felt comfortable. After a pause, a committee member added that if she had any interest in ministering to the pastors' spouses, it might be greatly appreciated.

The spouse took that suggestion seriously and developed several ways in which to add value to the pastors' spouses and increase their self-esteem. But the new executive and his wife never would have known that was a need—or an unexpressed expectation—had they not asked the question.

How Does the Church Expect to Compensate You?

What are the congregation's expectations for the pastor's compensation package? How will they handle Social Security reimbursement? Do they supply a parsonage or pastor's residence, or do they pay a housing allowance? If they supply a parsonage, do they also provide a cash equity allowance? What about car expenses, books and magazines, and continuing education? How often is the compensation package reviewed? By whom?

What does the congregation expect the pastor to do with his or her time? Do they anticipate their pastor will work forty hours a week? Sixty? Eighty? Do they expect home visits, hospital calls, nursing home visitation? Do they expect a pastor to work every evening, as well as eight hours a day?

When you seek clarification from the search committee, emulate Douglas Scott's practice: "I try not to sound judgmental; my tone suggests that I am merely acquiring information. They may have thought of the pastor's job only in the most general terms. These questions force them to state their expectations clearly both for themselves and the candidate."[2]

Expectations

"Churches want their pastors to be both cloistered, contemplative scholars and aggressive, decisive administrators. Other churches expect their pastor to have specialized skills (preaching or counseling or youth work) and yet be generalists competent in all areas."

—Richard P. Hansen[3]

Jesus Prepares Us

After three years of ministry on earth, Jesus knew he did not have much longer with his apostles. How did he prepare them for their next assignment, which was to form the first church and then lead it through its first few years of existence?

He gave them three great assurances that will serve us well, no matter what our next assignment may be.

You Will Receive Answers to Prayer

Jesus promised, "I will do whatever you ask in my name, so that the Son may bring glory to the Father. You may ask me for anything in my name, and I will do it" (John 14:13–14).

This sounds like a *carte blanche* promise. It's like giving your child a credit card and telling him or her, "Here, go get whatever you want. I'm good for it."

Naturally, Jesus is not promising to honor every selfish request we may think of asking, especially if we are presumptuous enough to ask for nonessential, material things. But he does love to answer prayer. If we ask in his name, and according to his will (1 John 5:14), we know that he hears us.

You Will Do Greater Things

Jesus told his followers, "I tell you the truth, anyone who has faith in me will do what I have been doing. He will do even greater things than these, because I am going to the Father" (John 14:12).

Imagine the response of the apostles upon hearing such a statement, that they will do even greater things than Jesus did. Think of all the miracles they had witnessed.

Of course, his prophecy came true. "In the first few months after his death and resurrection many more men and women became his followers through their witness than had done so during his personal ministry in Galilee and Judaea."[4]

You too will do greater things through your ministry. Think of the advantages you have: television, radio, e-mail, the Internet, social networking sites. The possibilities are almost unlimited.

Yet lest we think we can do greater things simply because we live in a more technologically advanced age, let me emphasize it is not because of these things alone. It is because of the presence and power of the Holy Spirit.

You Have the Presence and Power of the Holy Spirit

Jesus promised, "I will ask the Father, and he will give you another Counselor to be with you forever—the Spirit of truth" (John 14:16–17).

He is our helper. The word translated *counselor* denotes "one who is called alongside as a helper or defender, a friend at court."[5]

Jesus mentions "another counselor," which implies they already had one, namely Jesus himself. He was indeed their counselor, their defender, and their friend as he walked the dusty roads of Galilee and Judea. He is also our counselor and helper as he indwells us in the person of his Holy Spirit.

We enter a new assignment keenly aware of our need of this comforter. We would be foolish to enter any assignment without the consciousness that he is with us.

Perection or Infection?

"However much we may wish it otherwise, at conversion, divine perfection does not set in. But *divine infection* does. We have been invaded by the living God himself in the person of the Spirit whose goal is to infect us thoroughly with God's likeness."

—Gordon Fee[6]

He is our interpreter. Continuing the upper room discourse, Jesus also declares: "All this I have spoken while still with you. But the Counselor, the Holy Spirit, whom the Father will send in my name, will teach you all things and will remind you of everything I have said to you" (John 14:25–26).

Even while Jesus was with the apostles, they did not always fully understand the things he taught them. In their future ministry, the Holy Spirit would bring to mind the things they had heard, would reteach them the lessons, and would drive home the meaning, interpreting what they had heard.

We, too, need the Spirit's interpretation of the things we read in God's Word so that we may rightly express it to our congregation.

He is our witness. Jesus said: "When the Counselor comes, whom I will send to you from the Father, the Spirit of truth who goes out from the Father, he will testify about me. And you also must testify, for you have been with me from the beginning" (John 15:26–27).

When Peter and his colleagues stood before the Sanhedrin, they proclaimed the resurrection of Jesus. Peter said, "We are witnesses of these things, and so is the Holy Spirit, whom God has given to those who obey him" (Acts 5:32).

As we share the good news about Jesus Christ, how thrilling to know that he is strengthening us through the Holy Spirit to give witness to the truth about him and his way of salvation.

He is our prosecutor. Jesus knew the apostles' hearts would be filled with sorrow when he went away. So he assured them:

> But I tell you the truth: It is for your good that I am going away. Unless I go away, the Counselor will not come to you; but if I go, I will send him to you. When he comes, he will convict the world of guilt in regard to sin and righteousness and judgment: in regard to sin, because men do not believe in me; in regard to righteousness, because I am going to the Father, where you can see me no longer; and in regard to judgment, because the prince of this world now stands condemned. (John 16:7–11)

We do not have to convict the world of its sin and judgment. Our attempts fall flat and may even sound judgmental and intolerant. As we are faithful to declare his Word, he is faithful to prosecute those whose guilt prevents them from responding.

He is our revealer. Jesus said, "I have much more to say to you, more than you can now bear. But when he, the Spirit of truth, comes, he will guide you into all truth. He will not speak on his own; he will speak only what he hears, and he will tell you what is yet to come" (John 16:12–13).

Just as the disciples did not grasp everything Jesus taught, so we, too, have much to learn. Fortunately, God sends his Spirit to guide us into truth.

A minister was late coming to the pulpit one morning. Others had led the early parts of the worship service, assuming the pastor would come for the sermon. When he did not arrive on time, the congregation sat a few moments in embarrassing silence. Finally a side door opened, the pastor came in, and proceeded to the pulpit where he gave a powerful message.

When someone asked him later why he was tardy, he responded, "I was waiting in prayer for a few more moments. I told God I would not go to the pulpit unless he came with me."

We, too, must have the presence and power of God in the pulpit and in every other phase of ministry. Fortunately, Jesus has prepared us for that ministry by promising to answer our prayers in his name, by promising we will do greater things than he did, and by giving us the Holy Spirit to minister through us.

Preparing for the Interview

One of the most important ways you can get ready for your next assignment is to be prepared for the interview with the search committee. A colleague told me the chair of the search committee gave him a list of questions the committee would ask during the course of the interview. The good news was that they were thoughtful enough to give him the list. The bad news: They gave it to him only an hour before the meeting, so there was little time to digest all the committee wanted to know.

Yet many candidates never see a list of questions and must respond on the spot to whatever the committee asks. Breathing a prayer for wisdom and guidance is probably the best preparation for a time when you are on the hot seat.

Your Initiative in an Interview

You may want to make it clear in advance that you too will have some questions for the committee. One young pastor was interviewing for his first church. In a meeting with a search committee, he was too inexperienced to think of any questions. He was frankly just trying to find a job. When the committee asked him if he had any questions, he was embarrassed to admit he did not. In his defense, he felt the committee had been thorough in what they told him about the church, so he really did not have questions.

One of the members chuckled and said, "Don't you even want to know whether we're solvent?" He was so naïve, he wasn't sure what *solvent* meant, but he thought it had something to do with money, so he said, "I guess it would be good to know that." They proceeded to give him a brief report on the state of their finances, which was positive.

Doug Scott suggests your questions should be of three types:[7]

Census. What kinds of people attend the church? Does the church draw its members from the immediate vicinity surrounding the church? Have there been major demographic shifts in the immediate community in the past few years? Is housing in the area affordable for young couples?

One colleague faced such changing demographics. The church was located in an older neighborhood in a large metropolitan area. Most of the original homeowners had either died or moved to the suburbs. However, this negative was offset with a positive: the housing, although older, was affordable as starter homes for young couples, thus providing the church with new potential.

Issues. Is the church wrangling over worship? Is the church outreach-minded or is it ingrown? Are there theological divisions in the church? Under what conditions did the former pastor leave? How are church budgets formed? Is this a source of contention or division?

Structures. How is church business transacted? Is it strongly congregational or lead by the board? How is the board chosen? That may be decided by a predetermined polity, but it is surprising how creative some churches become, within proscribed limits.

What is the history of the relationship of the board with its pastor? Who runs the programs of the church? For instance, who is responsible for spiritual formation programs, youth ministries, children's ministries? Who oversees building maintenance?

How supportive is the church of its denomination? If it is an independent church, does it cooperate with a local clergy association?

Other Areas to Explore

You might want to ask why the church is particularly interested in you. It's possible they really are not if your name was given by a bishop or superintendent and they are simply fulfilling an obligation.

You might ask about significant events in the life of the congregation. The answers will tell you what is important to the person who answers, but it may also reveal the kind of ministries this congregation values.

You might also inquire as to what the former pastor did well. What were the circumstances surrounding his or her departure?

What is the church's mission statement? Vision statement? Goals?

You will never find out everything about a church during the interview, just as they will never find out everything about you. But going into it with some preparation will provide better information than you might otherwise learn.

Tips on Preparing

A few do's and don'ts may be helpful in preparing for your next church.

Don't Take Your Baggage with You

Your luggage, yes, but not your baggage. If you have had a disappointing experience in your current church, if you are leaving under duress, or if you feel you have been mistreated, try to put those issues behind you before you take up your new assignment. This is not easy. I'm not aware of any pill that will help us go to sleep miserable and wake up happy.

You may need to confide in a trusted friend or counselor. Talking through what happened and especially how you feel about what happened is an important step toward healing. Being courageous enough to admit your own fault in whatever happened is another. In the spirit of Matthew 5:23–24, try to mend fences with those toward whom you have bad feelings.

You don't want to start a new ministry with a cloud over your head from the last one.

Don't Depend Too Heavily on Previous Sermons

Admittedly, it can be a lifesaver in a new parish to have a supply of sermons to help you through the first few weeks. With so many adjustments, so many new things to learn and new people to meet, with getting your home settled and into livable condition, it can be a stress-reducer to utilize previously used material. If the truth you preached in the past helped others, it is still truth and will help others in a different place.

Yet, you must not learn to depend solely on your previous research. Think about it: if you develop no new sermons, when you come to the bottom of your sermon barrel, you will have to move again!

A more important reason not to rely on past research is that digging for new sermons will keep you fresh. It will keep your illustrations current. It will make your messages more relevant to your new congregation. And you will become more excited about newly discovered truth. It will show in your presentation.

Don't Assume that What Worked There Will Work Here

One of the problems in going to pastors' conferences and hearing about someone else's success is assuming that what worked for them will work for you. I have conducted many conferences around the country, but I have tried to share principles, not fads. I have tried to recommend transferrable concepts, not methods that are localized in a particular community.

When you move from one parish to another, and especially from one part of the country to another, you will discover the needs of the congregation are different. For instance, sections of the Midwest have a stronger work ethic and stronger family values than you may find in other parts of the country.

A promotional program or theme that worked well in your current congregation may fall flat in the next one. A study group or emphasis that fizzled in your present parish may ignite and be wildly successful in your next church. The point is: Don't assume that responses will be the same. They almost certainly won't.

Do Secure a Directory of Your New Church's Families

If you can possibly procure a directory of your new parish, it will help you immensely in getting to know people, both before you arrive and after you are there. From the outset, you will have pictures and contact information for most of your families. This gives you a head start in forming relationships with your new friends.

Planning

"He who every morning plans the transaction of the day and follows out that plan, carries a thread that will guide him through the maze of the most busy life. But where no plan is laid, where the disposal of time is surrendered merely to the chance of incidence, chaos will soon reign."

—Victor Hugo[8]

Do Find Out Who the Leaders Are

Rest assured that when you arrive in your new parish, you will not be the leader. You will have a position, but someone else will be the leader. Even though you may initiate board meetings, craft agendas, supervise staff, and go through all the motions of a leader, someone else will be the influential leader of the church.

Leadership is influence. Find out who the influential leaders are and work with them. When a colleague arrived in his new church, a distant relative, who also happened to be a member of the church, told him, "Watch out for Bill Smith. He's a church boss."

My colleague considered this advice, but was wise enough to recognize that Bill Smith was an influential leader in the congregation. He was not only on his church board, but also occupied seats on several boards in the community. In addition, he was active on denominational boards.

My friend thought, "I don't know if he's a church boss or not, but I think it will be wise if I become his friend." He did and they had a great relationship. No one was a greater supporter than the man characterized as a church boss.

> **Preparation**
>
> "Forewarned, forearmed; to be prepared is half the victory."
>
> —Miguel de Cervantes[9]

This is not political manipulation; it is wisdom. It recognizes that only after you have earned people's respect and trust will they truly allow you to lead. If you gain the trust of those who are already influential leaders and they throw their support behind you, others will follow.

Be Prepared

An old story tells about a college student who was failing all his courses. Finally, the administration terminated him and kicked him out of school. Fearful of what his parents would think and say and do, he sent a telegram to his mother: "I've been kicked out of school. Prepare Pop."

His mother's reply was to the point: "Pop prepared. Prepare yourself."

That's exactly what we must do, to the best of our ability. We cannot know everything, but we will know more and be better prepared if we do our homework. As Whitney Young, Jr., said, "It is better to be prepared for an opportunity and not have one than to have an opportunity and not be prepared."[10]

Action Steps

1. Take some time to remember your first impressions of your present church. How accurate did they prove to be? Were you prepared? What could you have done to prepare yourself better for this church?
2. How well did you clarify expectations before coming to this church? What surprises have you had? What about things you didn't expect but they did? Or things you did expect and they did not?

8

Mentoring
Preparing Your Current Congregation for Transition

You can prepare your congregation for your departure or you can just let it happen. Either choice has consequences.

I've gradually learned how to leave properly, so that with the tension there is also a sense of joy.
—Robert Kemper

Pastor Steve rummaged through the workroom closet adjacent to the church office. He hadn't found a new volunteer secretary yet. His first week on the job had been filled with getting acquainted, attending a lovely reception provided for him and his family, and making several calls at the hospital to minister to a terminally ill patient.

The church could not afford to hire a secretary, not even a part-time person. So Steve would have to do the bulletin himself this week. He knew the bulletin stock must be in the closet somewhere, but where?

On one shelf he discovered a small stack of bulletins already printed, left over from his predecessor's last Sunday at the church. The former pastor had inserted a farewell paragraph on page 3. "We have invested six years of our lives with you," the message began. "There have been some good accomplishments, but apparently not enough. Some people don't seem to be satisfied with our relocating from the rundown building and community we left downtown. This beautiful new church building in a growing community should be enough to make anyone happy. I have done my best. I regret that it was not good enough for some people."

"Wow!" Steve thought. "I understood he left rather unwillingly, but I didn't realize how bitter he was about it." He looked around the office, walked out into the hall, and stood at the door to the sanctuary. The church was beautiful. His predecessor had done an outstanding job of leading the congregation through a major building program. He and the building committee had thought of every detail. It was a great place to worship.

But what a way to leave a church! Steve wondered how much bitterness still resided in the congregation—or had the pastor taken it all with him? Maybe those dissatisfied with the former pastor just breathed a collective sigh of relief that he was gone.

The Struggles in Leaving

Apparently Steve's predecessor did not think about how he was preparing the congregation (or not) for his departure. We'll deal with that more specifically later in this chapter. But part of the preparation is to understand what both you and the congregation are going through.

Leaving a church is difficult in almost any situation. If things have gone well in your pastorate, it may break your heart to leave people you love, with whom you have partnered in the ministry, and in whom you have invested a significant portion of your life.

I know . . . I just left a wonderful church in Oklahoma City after thirteen years of pastoral ministry. No pastor could have served a better church. The most loving, caring, and supportive congregation in the universe. But, as I write this book, six months have gone by since my farewell service and they recently installed a new pastor named Kent Hubbard. Because he was my executive pastor for many years at Trinity, he asked me to speak at his installation service. What an awesome experience. I stayed out of the search process and yet was thrilled to see the church full and the anticipation of a great future with a wonderful new pastor.

On the other hand, if things have not gone well, it's easy to be filled with regret. It's hard not to blame yourself that things didn't go better. The temptation is to make a long list of the things that might have been if only you had tried harder, prayed more, or worked more diligently. Or maybe you're relieved to escape! But then, especially if you feel some people have mistreated you, you have to be careful not to walk away with bitterness.

In any case, you're bound to have conflicting emotions. Robert Kemper said leaving a church reminded him of the fable of the tortoise and the hare. In fact, at times he felt like both the tortoise and the hare.[1]

The Tortoise and the Hare

Like the tortoise, he was getting ready to move, carrying everything he owned with him. Not literally on his back like the tortoise, but the image was close enough, whether loading possessions into a U-Haul or watching professionals pack it into a large moving van.

On the other hand, like the hare, he was rushing into the future. A new parish awaited him. New doors of ministry were about to open. At such a time, the present seems like a barrier. Every fiber of the pastor's being wants to get on with the new assignment.

You run the risk of leaving before you leave. You're still the pastor until the last day. So be prepared for your emotions to rise and fall, run ahead and retreat, as you work through leaving in an appropriate way.

Then there are the memories. When a congregation decides to relocate, one of the great hindrances is all the memories people have of wonderful things that happened in the old building. They remember weddings, baby dedications or baptisms, perhaps their own baptism, or some other high spiritual moment.

What many pastors don't stop to think about until it smacks them in the forehead is their own memories in a parish. You officiated at those weddings and baptisms, you preached from that pulpit, you counseled in that office, sharing moments of confession with counselees who trusted you. You married and buried; you wept with those who wept and rejoiced with those who rejoiced. You have your own memories to work through as you approach the time to leave.

The Real Reasons for Leaving

Then, of course, people often won't understand your reasons for leaving. You may not even understand all the reasons yourself—at least not now.

"Are you getting paid more money in your new church?" someone asked one of my colleagues. After all, isn't that why people leave one job and go to the next, to get more money or better benefits?

"This move will take you back home, closer to your family, right?" a parishioner asked another colleague. That's another reason people change jobs, right? They want to be near aging parents or growing grandchildren or other family members.

I hope you do get paid more money in your next parish. And if you are now a long distance from your family, I hope the next move takes you closer. But, of course, most ministers want to go where God wants them to be. That's the first and foremost reason for moving. Sincere pastors will often agonize over the decision, trying to put selfish motivations in the background, so they can hear the voice of God more clearly and sense his direction.

If You Don't Love Jesus . . .

"If you don't love Jesus you will soon discover that being a pastor or a church leader is not really a very good job. You will be overworked, underpaid, overstressed, and underappreciated. But if you do love Jesus, you will discover as so many others have that it can be the most wonderful and exciting job in the world."

—Mark Allan Powell[2]

But no matter how much you share with your congregation about your passion for God's will, no matter how "spiritual" you try to make your decision sound, there will be some who will not understand. They will attribute some "unspiritual" reason to your move, like money or family or even a political move to advance your career. Love them anyway, and do your best to obey the voice of God.

Living What You Preach

We read one of the great farewell messages of the Bible in Acts chapter 20, when Paul told the Ephesian elders goodbye. Sailing from Troas to Jerusalem, Paul decided to bypass

Ephesus because he was in a hurry (Acts 20:16), but he wanted to see the elders of the Ephesian church. So he arranged to meet them in Miletus, a few miles down the coast.

Live with Humility

Once the elders were assembled, Paul told them, "You know how I lived the whole time I was with you, from the first day I came into the province of Asia. I served the Lord with great humility and with tears" (Acts 20:18–19).

A Relevant Message

"The challenge we face as clergy is to make our message relevant. Look closely at what you do and how you do it. Love your people. Be a shepherd to them. Get out in the village and refuse to be desk-bound. Watch your life and your doctrine closely. Don't be easily swayed by every new concept. Play to your strength. Preach the Word. And, at any cost, stay pure!!"

—H. B. London[3]

Pastors prepare their congregations for their departure long before they leave. How you live your life among them is part of how you prepare them. You can live with arrogance, as if the success of the church depends solely upon you and your gifts. Or you can live humbly, recognizing you are replaceable.

When Knute Larson was considering a move to a different church, he turned on the radio and heard the associate director of the program explain why he was leaving the broadcast. The man said, "I have struggled with the issue of my indispensability. But I've come to the conclusion that God can replace me in this ministry. The work here will go on, so I must take this next step in my life."[4]

If you live with this humble attitude, you are more likely to train your parishioners to use their gifts. You are more likely to develop leaders. You are more likely to form a team rather than a one-person show. In all these ways, you are preparing them for your departure.

Preach Faithfully

Paul also told the Ephesian elders, "You know that I have not hesitated to preach anything that would be helpful to you but have taught you publicly and from house to house. . . . For I have not hesitated to proclaim to you the whole will of God" (Acts 20:20, 27).

In other words, he discipled them. He consciously added to their spiritual formation. His preaching was not intended to make them feel good, but to strengthen them. He avoided those who would "gather around them a great number of teachers to say what their itching ears want to hear" (2 Tim. 4:3). Instead Paul modeled the advice he gave Timothy: "But you, keep your head in all situations, endure hardship, do the work of an evangelist, discharge all the duties of your ministry" (2 Tim. 4:5).

Effective Preaching

"Put salvation on the table. Talk straight about sin. Pull no punches about judgment. Make the blood of Christ your turning point, and issue a lavish invitation to grace. Make it plain; that's the preacher's job."[5]

When you leave, you will know you did your best to build their character and their devotion to God through your preaching.

Challenge Them Boldly

Paul challenged the Ephesians, "Keep watch over yourselves and all the flock of which the Holy Spirit has made you overseers. Be shepherds of the church of God, which he bought with his own blood" (Acts 20:28).

In other words, he urged them to take care of themselves. It had been some time since Paul had actually ministered among the Ephesians. Their current pastor may have been among the elders he addressed that day in Miletus. But he looked all of them in the eyes and urged them to stand together against the enemy of their souls.

A colleague told me about accepting the pastorate of a church that had gone for more than two years without a senior pastor. Normally it would be devastating for a church to go that long without a leader. Fortunately, a predecessor had taught them to care for themselves. They had a system of small groups and small group leaders who watched over their mini-congregations. Although their attendance suffered, the core group remained strong. Someone had taught them to take care of each other.

Move on Confidently

In a moment of frank vulnerability, Paul said, "And now, compelled by the Spirit, I am going to Jerusalem, not knowing what will happen to me there" (Acts 20:22).

This was not a whine, nor was it a complaint. Paul was not looking for sympathy. We can certainly read between the lines and believe he was asking for their prayers as he faced an unknown future.

In ancient times, when cartographers made maps of their explorations, they would inevitably come to a point on the map beyond which they were not confident. They didn't know what was out there, so they would write phrases such as "Here be dragons" or "Here be demons."

But Sir John Franklin, a master mariner in the days of King Henry V, used a different method. On his maps, he crossed out the dismal phrases "Here be dragons" and "Here be demons." In their place he wrote "Here is God."[6]

Paul knew, whatever else was awaiting him in Jerusalem, God was there. What an example for the Ephesian elders. Departing pastors are wise to express such confidence in God's plan, both for themselves and for the church.

Commit Them to God with Assurance

Paul left no doubt as to who would take care of the Ephesians. He told them, "Now I commit you to God and to the word of his grace, which can build you up and give you an inheritance among all those who are sanctified" (Acts 20:32).

What Paul was really saying is this: "What God originates, he orchestrates."[7]

The same God who was calling Paul to move on to the next adventure was the God who would provide grace for the Ephesians, build them up, and give them a rich inheritance.

So not only in the way he said goodbye, but also in the way he preached and taught and lived among them, Paul prepared the Ephesians for his departure.

Preparing Your Final Message

In 1792, as George Washington approached the end of his first term as president of the United States, he asked James Madison to put together some notes he could use in preparing his farewell address. When Washington decided not to retire at the end of one term, he put the notes aside until 1796, when he took them out again in preparation for his impending retirement.

After preparing a first draft of his speech, Washington gave it to Alexander Hamilton and suggested he revise it. Over a period of four months, Washington and Hamilton exchanged various drafts of the speech. At one point, Hamilton showed his version of the farewell address to John Jay. When Washington finally wrote his final version, it was admittedly a collaborative effort. But he and his advisors succeeded in capturing the president's thoughts and principles, which he then communicated to the American public.

Attempt Big Things

"We dare to attempt big things for God. We dare to be holy. We dare to be obedient. We dare, because we know the eternal arms of God will hold us if we fall."

—Juan Carlos Ortiz[8]

Washington did not give his speech orally and personally. Instead he arranged for a Philadelphia newspaper to publish it. In the days and weeks that followed, other newspapers in the new republic also published it.[9]

Few pastors make their farewell sermon a collaborative event. But a pastor should prepare the final message to the congregation with great care and deliberation. Not to be morbid, but like the final words a person says before dying, they are of great importance.

The final message helps to set a tone for a pastor's departure. A bitter reminiscence leaves a bad taste in the mouth and is out of place. A syrupy, sweet reminiscence that recites the pastor's accomplishments or a sad lamentation, bemoaning the soon departure of the pastor and family, are equally out of place.

Be Positive

Instead, be positive in your final comments. In most cases, enough good things have happened over the years of your tenure that you shouldn't have any problem being positive. Let the congregation know it has been a pleasure to serve with them. Of course, if that is not the case, don't say so.

If you're leaving in less than desirable circumstances, you don't need to be dishonest in your comments. But take the high road. Don't denigrate anyone. When your world crumbles, you don't have to be one of the crumbs.

Scott Simpson is a professional golfer who has played often at the Masters Golf Tournament in Augusta, Georgia. To play at the Augusta National is so beautiful; it is like walking into an oil painting. Simpson told his caddie, "You won't see a weed all week."

After five days of walking the course, his caddie pointed to the ground and announced, "I found one!"[10]

Your experience at your church may not have been as pristine as walking the Augusta National, but you don't have to be like the caddie and find a flaw just for the sake of pointing it out.

Be Complimentary

In all likelihood, most of the people of your church have been faithful and cooperative. You ought to say so.

Lee Strobel remembers his father's death in 1979, while Lee was in law school. He flew back for the wake, and one of his father's friends stopped by to greet him. He said, "Are you Wally's son? Oh, he was so proud of you. He used to brag about you all the time. When you went off to Yale Law School, he was just thrilled." Lee was stunned because he had no idea his father felt that way.

His dad's friend continued. "When you'd have a byline in the *Tribune*, he was always showing it to everybody. He couldn't stop talking about you! You were such an important part of his life."

Strobel says he wonders what their relationship would have been like if his father had said those things himself while they still had time together.[11]

Be sure your people know how much you love and appreciate them. Don't wait until you leave to tell them. But, by all means, be sure you express it then.

Be Inspiring

When Ronald Reagan gave his farewell address to the nation on January 11, 1989, he waxed eloquent:

> I've spoken of the shining city all my political life . . . And how stand [*sic*] the city on this winter night? . . . After two hundred years, two centuries, she still stands strong and true on the granite ridge, and her glow has held steady no matter what storm. And she's still a beacon, still a magnet for all who must have freedom, for all the pilgrims from all the lost places who are hurtling through the darkness, toward home.[12]

Those are inspiring words. You too can be inspiring. After all, your church is a light in a dark place. It's like a city on a hill. Whether you call it a lighthouse, a hospital for healing the spiritually wounded, or a safe place in the storm, be inspiring. In your final message, encourage the people and lift up the church as providing the best hope in the world for meeting the deepest needs of humanity.

Your Exit Strategy

What is your exit strategy for leaving your church? Usually, the term *exit strategy* has negative overtones, because it is considered "a means of escaping one's current situation, typically an unfavourable situation. . . . At worst, an exit strategy will save face; at best, an exit strategy will peg a withdrawal to the achievement of an objective worth more than the cost of continued involvement."[13]

People inside the Pentagon used the term *exit strategy* during the Vietnam War, but it came into more popular usage during the Battle of Mogadishu, Somalia. U.S. soldiers lost their lives in the U.N. peacekeeping activities there when our country did not seem to have a clear objective for being involved.

The term need not be negative. It can simply mean being intentional about leaving and having a plan for doing it well. There are several elements that can make your leaving the church more positive.

Leave Good Records

If you have the luxury of knowing you will leave several weeks before you actually do, you can make a diligent effort to leave the church records and historical information in satisfactory form for the next pastor.

When Orval Butcher left Skyline Wesleyan Church in Lemon Grove, California, over his final six months he concentrated on updating records in eight areas.[14]

Membership records. Butcher and his secretary endeavored to bring all data up to date regarding members received, withdrawn, dismissed, or deceased.

Weddings, baby dedications, and baptisms. These records were also updated.

Check for accuracy. They did this primarily through phone calls where there were questions.

Photos and slides. Today these would probably be digitized, but where are they and how does one access them?

Sunday bulletins and weekly mailers. These may be stored electronically, but the church may also have hard copies stored.

Current information on members. This data must all be updated.

Records of board actions. A capable volunteer, with time and an eye for detail, could scrutinize board minutes and compile actions to keep future boards from duplicating work that has already been done.

Job descriptions for paid staff members. Staff assignments often evolve over the course of time and it is helpful to update these.

As pastors come and go, these records, properly maintained, become important in the life of the church, preserving its history and chronicling its progress.

Affirm the Choice of a New Leader

If you remain neutral when you should be supportive, your nonsupport becomes a negative factor and is hurtful to the cause.

Prepare Your Final Message Carefully

We talked about this earlier, but I include it here because it is such an important part of preparing the congregation for your departure. Choose a great passage of Scripture and affirm that the ministry of the church will continue after you have gone. Or develop a short series of messages that will call the church to be faithful to its mission and vision, to be supportive of the new pastor, and to glorify God with its ministry.

Three Choices

As a resigning pastor you have three choices:

1. You can openly support the incoming pastor.
2. You can openly oppose him or her.
3. You can remain neutral.

—Orval Butcher[15]

You can't accomplish everything in one last sermon or one last series, so be realistic. If you haven't accomplished all you would like to do at that church, you probably can't make up for it on the final Sunday.

Even Billy Graham, who has preached for more than fifty years on radio and television and in stadiums all over the world, believes he preaches the most misunderstood message ever. If you ask the person on the street what Billy Graham says is the way to heaven, the vast majority will say "you need to live a good life, follow the Golden Rule, make positive choices, be nice to people, and do the right things. But," Dr. Graham stresses, "I've never preached that. I preach the opposite."[16] He explains that he has stressed salvation is the gift of God through Jesus Christ and no one can earn it by good works.

Even if people on the street misunderstand, most of your congregation will appreciate the sum total of your teaching over the years. This is why your final message must not be a last-ditch effort to correct all the mistakes or misunderstandings. It must be a noble effort at glorifying God, elevating the Church, and expressing confidence in the future.

Let People Love You

People will want to express themselves to you before you leave. Most will have warm words of appreciation for your ministry. You must let them do this. Some will want to give you gifts that are meaningful to them. Accept them graciously. It is their way of giving thanks for your ministry.

The congregation may also give some kind of farewell party or celebration of your ministry. This too is important. As Kemper points out, "The proper word for all these festivities is *closure*. Endings need to be formalized in some way. First, they mark the new chapter in my life. Second, they clear out debris for the church, so it can make a fresh beginning."[17]

Lovingly Sever Relationships

The hardest part of leaving a church is leaving people you have grown to love and who love you. You may find some people will be angry at you for leaving. They may be angry at your denominational system for moving you or angry at specific executives who had something to do with your change of church assignments.

You may receive phone calls, e-mails, or notes from people who have a hard time expressing themselves in person. These are often painful exchanges, but as lovingly and sensitively as possible, you sever relationships and move on.

You may keep in touch by exchanging Christmas greetings or other appropriate correspondence from time to time. But as we said in chapter six, you will want to leave and not return for a lengthy season in order to allow your successor to become well-established.

The Final Words

None of us likes to be caught unprepared. Even an experienced public speaker hates to hear those words, "Tom, come up here and say a few words."

In a similar way, you don't want to enter the final weeks of your tenure without thinking about how you want to end this phase of your ministry. You have a responsibility to prepare yourself and your congregation for this time.

Regarding the importance of preparation, former heavyweight champion Joe Frazier said, "You can map out a fight plan or a life plan. But when the action starts, you're down to your reflexes. That's where your roadwork shows. If you cheated on that in the dark of the morning, you're getting found out now under the bright lights."[18]

By thoughtfully preparing your congregation for your departure, you will give them confidence to step into the next phase of the church's life and ministry. You can walk away, knowing you did not cheat either them or yourself in the final days.

Action Steps

1. Think through what records need to be updated before you leave. Who will you ask to help with this important task?
2. Make a list of the things you want to be sure to say before you leave, either in a final message or in a series of messages.

9

Family

Preparing Those You Love for Transition

Moving from one church to another has a major impact on the pastor's spouse and children.

Like a shepherd's tent my house has been pulled down and taken from me.
—Isaiah 38:12

"It's not fair, Dad! It's totally not fair!"

"I realize this is hard, son, but I've tried to explain that I just feel like it's the right thing to do. I think I'm a good fit for that church and now is the time to move."

"But all my friends! I have nine guys who are my age at church. Why do I have to leave my friends just so you can obey God? Doesn't he care about what I want?"

Mitch turned away and looked out the car window as they passed the community swimming pool. It was packed with young people, trying to cool off in the late August heat.

Turning back to his father, he said, "I was really looking forward to football this fall. You know our team only lost one game last year and I know it's a stretch, but I might even make varsity as a sophomore. You say we're not leaving until November, so what's the point in even going out for football here? And by the time we move, it will be too late to get involved at the new school. Not that I would have a chance. I don't know them and they don't know me! The whole thing stinks!"

"You know, frankly, I don't understand the timing either. But God has a way of working things out. You remember it was hard when we moved here, but you made new friends and it's been a great experience for you."

"Well, I don't really remember all that much about that move. I was only in third grade, you know!"

They drove in silence the rest of the way home. Pastor Glen knew he would have to work hard to keep the lines of communication open with Mitch. They were going to move, but he didn't want to lose his son in the process. This was going to take a lot of prayer.

Stages of Grief in Transitioning

As I pointed out briefly in chapter 6, a pastor's move to a new congregation has a significant impact on the parsonage family. While it's an adjustment for the pastor, he or she has a new challenge waiting, and the pastor usually adjusts to the transition more quickly than either the spouse or the children.

Christine threw herself across the bed and began to sob into her pillow. Her dad had just told the family they were moving more than five hundred miles away. She would have to leave her beloved Franklin High School just before her senior year. She would have to transition from a student body of nearly three thousand, with its many clubs and activities to a small town high school of less than two hundred fifty, with a senior class of no more than sixty.

She just couldn't stand the thought of being uprooted from her friends, her church, her school, and her life! Surely her father was making a mistake. She had heard the church in the new community was very strict and the whole area was more conservative. How would she ever survive?

It isn't just the children who suffer. Spouses struggle with the change of venue as well. One pastor's wife said, "My entire root system is gone! I feel like a plant that has been pulled from fertile soil, then left to shrivel up and die. This feeling of rootlessness is overwhelming me. I just want to be put back in that pot, packed with soil, and fertilized!"[1]

Passing through Grief

"The Scriptures see grief as a normal part of the life process. Groping through your own grief is an emotional, physical, and spiritual effort. Faith gives us the power to pass through grief, not avoid it."

—Billy Graham[2]

We shouldn't be surprised that people feel uprooted when they have to move away from familiar surroundings and be thrust into a new environment. And it isn't just pastoral families who face such adjustments. It happens to military families as well as people who work in government or business. No family, it seems, is immune from the possibility of being uprooted.

Counselors tell us that leaving a church is much like losing a loved one. It's like going through a divorce or experiencing a funeral of someone dear to us. They also tell us that we go through stages in the grief process. Without question, a pastor's family faces some of those stages.

Denial

Maybe it was denial that caused Mitch, in our opening story, to retreat when he moved to the new community. He did not physically retreat. He went to school and to church, but he seemed to retreat emotionally. He refused to get involved at school beyond attending classes. Although youth leaders at the new church tried to involve him in their activities, he was slow to come around.

A pastor's spouse may be reluctant to make friends in a new place. After all, he or she has just had several friendships, perhaps some very close ones, jerked away. Why go through the pain of making new friends only to have them torn away in a few years?

Anger

Christine was very angry with her father for making the decision to move. She felt abandoned, disregarded. Did he ask her how she felt about relocating? No, he just announced to the family that they were moving. Did anyone care about her feelings? Nobody seemed to. Although she would never challenge her father outwardly, inwardly she seethed with resentment.

Far across the country, Pastor Gerald and his wife, Kathy, drove two hundred miles to candidate at a rural church searching for a pastor. Gerald had served as an associate, but this would be his first church all on his own. Three days after he had visited the church and interviewed for the position, the chair of the board telephoned to say they had decided to call him.

When he told Kathy about it, she became very quiet. "Aren't you excited?" he asked. "This is the opportunity I've been waiting for."

Kathy remained silent.

"What's wrong?" he asked.

She spoke without looking directly at him. "I'm not ready to move. We have family here in the area. I'm not ready to pull up roots and move to a new community."

"What? Why didn't you tell me that's the way you felt before I candidated and built up their hopes as well as mine?"

"I didn't want to hurt your feelings by throwing cold water on your dream. You seemed so excited about it. But to be honest, I didn't think they would call you."

"You didn't think they would call me? So what is it? You don't think I'm qualified? You don't think I'm competent? How could you do this to me?"

He stalked out of the room, too angry to continue, too upset to wait for an answer.

Anger. It's frequently part of the grieving process, whether you move or whether you're disappointed you have to stay.

Depression

It may come amid packing the dishes. It may come when you pull out of the driveway of your old house for the last time. It may come when you wake up in the new house and realize you're not going back.

The Many Names of Depression

Depression goes by many names. John Bunyan called it the "slough of despond." Soldiers call it "battle fatigue." A weary businessman may call it "burnout." Psychiatrists might call it "anxiety neurosis." A layman may call it "nervous exhaustion."

The finality sets in. The decision is irrevocable. There's no turning back. And that realization often brings depression to the pastor's family.

If that's where you are, you are not alone. Even otherwise well-adjusted people sometimes become afflicted with the "black dog," as Churchill called it. William James, a pioneer of American psychology, faced a time of depression in which he was torn by doubts and fears. Afterward, he quoted an evangelist friend, Henry Aline, who had gone through a similar experience: "The fear was so invasive and powerful that if I had not clung to Scripture texts like, 'The eternal God is my refuge' or 'I am the resurrection and the life,' I think I would have gone really insane."[3]

Most pastors' families find the spiritual strength they need by ultimately trusting God and discovering that his providential leading brings them out into a better place. Even dark clouds often have silver linings.

Acceptance

Most pastors' families are troupers. They adjust. They learn to accept what they cannot change. They learn to overcome the "Lucy syndrome." You remember Lucy from the *Peanuts* comic strip. She and Charlie Brown were talking about the ballgame. She explained why she missed the ball. She said, "I remembered all the others I've missed . . . the past got in my eyes!"[4]

Pastors' spouses and children eventually learn to get the past out of their eyes, look to the future, and trust God. But it doesn't always come easily, and it seldom comes without a struggle.

An Ancient Family's Transition

If we could have been flies on the wall in the house of Abram, we would have learned a great deal about the trauma a family experiences when they pack up lock, stock, and barrel, and move to a strange country.

Unfortunately, no fly listened in, or if he did, he failed to write it down. No scribe sneaked in the back door and eavesdropped on Abram and Sarai's conversation. Yet, having studied human nature for many years, it isn't too hard for us to imagine what might have been said.

"The Lord God told you to do what? And leave whom? And go where?" Sarai must have said it. What self-respecting woman would not ask, especially "Sarah, who obeyed Abraham and called him her master" (1 Pet. 3:6)? The writer does not tell us about her inner struggles and what it took for her to get to the point where she said, "Yes, Abram, I will follow you wherever you go."

It would be another thousand years or so before Ruth uttered those memorable words to her mother-in-law: "Where you go I will go, and where you stay I will stay. Your people will be my people and your God my God" (Ruth 1:16). Countless adoring brides—including many pastors' wives—have recited those words to their handsome grooms, having little or no idea what lay in store for them.

If we don't know what happened behind the closed doors of Abram's home in Ur, we know with certainty that they moved—twice. First from Ur to Haran and later from Haran to Canaan. It was very much a family thing. In the first move, Terah seems to have taken the initiative: "Terah took his son Abram, his grandson Lot son of Haran, and his daughter-in-law Sarai, the wife of his son Abram, and together they set out from Ur of the Chaldeans to go to Canaan" (Gen. 11:31).

In all likelihood, since the inhabitants of both Ur and Haran worshiped the moon god and since Terah was probably an idolater, he felt at home in either place.[5] Yet, while Terah led the caravan, we know the move was God's idea. Before Abraham left Ur, "while he was still in Mesopotamia, before he lived in Haran" (Acts 7:2), God spoke to him. "Leave your country and your people," God had said, "and go to the land I will show you" (Acts 7:3).

Perhaps Abram influenced his father to move from Ur. But when the time came to migrate from Haran to Canaan, God had instructed Abraham, "Leave your country, your people and your father's household and go to the land I will show you" (Gen. 12:1).

In 1887, John Sammis penned the familiar lines:

> Trust and obey, for there's no other way
> To be happy in Jesus, but to trust and obey.

Trust and obey. More than 3,800 years before the inspired poet wrote those words, Abram lived them. In fact, they're the first two rules of a pastoral move—not only for the pastor, but also for the parsonage family.

Trust

Abram stepped out in faith—and so did Sarai. Maybe her faith was placed more in Abram than in God, but she was not the last spouse to so trust her husband. The truth is, neither one of them knew all the details about where they were going.

> By faith Abraham, when called to go to a place he would later receive as his inheritance, obeyed and went, *even though he did not know where he was going*. By faith he made his home in the promised land *like a stranger in a foreign country.* (Heb. 11:8–9, emphasis added)

Abraham is the patron saint of pastors and their families because we never know all the details about a new parish. No matter how many questions the search committee asks you or how many you ask them, you will begin your pastorate "like a stranger in a foreign country." You and they will learn many things about each other. And like Sarah, who followed her husband, your family will have many adjustments to make in a new land.

Obey

Without knowing all the details, Abraham obeyed. We don't know what their home looked like in Ur, nor in Haran. But we do know what their home was like in Canaan—it was a tent! The four walls were likely made of animal hides pieced together, or tightly woven cloth, not bricks and mortar. Today we call that roughing it!

Did he struggle with an attitude about leaving his family and moving to a strange place? Did Sarah? Most of us struggle with leaving our comfort zones and going to an unfamiliar place. But to do that in spite of our reservations is called obedience.

When Elisabeth Elliot was twelve years old, she told the Lord she wanted him to work out his will in her life at any cost. When he set about doing that very thing, she was amazed. She didn't think things would turn out the way they did.[6]

That's the way most of us are. God surprises us by calling us to do things we never dreamed of doing. But in the end, his way is better, higher, and greater than we could have imagined.

Hope

Something in Abraham hoped for the future. Although he lived in a tent, "he was looking forward to the city with foundations, whose architect and builder is God" (Heb. 11:10). When we make a move as a family, we have high hopes. We visualize our children growing up in the new place. We hope the schools will prove to be good and inspire our children to learn and grow. We hope the new church will be a place of Christian love, vision, and outreach, a place where our family will mature and flourish.

As the pastor's family moves to a new church, in spite of all the unknown factors, the known factor is God. With him, we will triumph.

Never Hopeless

"God believes in me. Therefore my situation is never hopeless.

"God walks with me. Therefore I am never alone.

"God is on my side. Therefore I can never lose."

—author unknown

Moving Affective Disorder

People who live in northern climates, who face short days and long nights in the late fall and winter, become acquainted with SAD—seasonal affective disorder. Some call it cabin fever. It's when the lack of sunshine, the cooler temperatures, and the shorter days begin to "trigger feelings of depression, lethargy, fatigue and other problems."[7]

People who face a move, with all the sorting, tossing, packing, unpacking, all the physical labor involved, as well as the emotional trauma of leaving a familiar place, become acquainted with MAD—moving affective disorder.[8]

MAD is not limited to pastoral families, but they are certainly among the prime candidates for it. Thousands face it each year as U-Haul trailers and moving vans back up to parsonages and load and unload their precious cargo.

Most of us want to handle it well. We want to stay calm. We want to be content during this difficult time, because usually we feel motivated by some sense that either God or the church or both have asked us to relocate.

The picture, magnetized and stuck to the refrigerator, showed a penguin under an umbrella on a tropical island. Sitting on an ice cube and sipping iced tea, the bird in a tuxedo was the picture of contentment. In fact, the caption beneath the picture declared, "For I have learned, in whatever *state* I am, to be content," a paraphrase of Paul's declaration from Philippians 4:11.[9]

The contented penguin is the ideal. It's what we hope to achieve. Anyone who tells you that's the way they feel all during a move, both leading up to it and during it, will lie to you about other things too!

A more apt illustration comes from the writing of Paul Tournier:

> I thought of the trapeze artists, swinging on their trapezes high up under the dome of the circus tent. They must let go of one trapeze just at the right moment, to hover for a moment in the void before catching hold of the other trapeze. As you watch, you identify yourself with them and experience the anxiety of the middle of the way, when they have let go of their first support and have not yet seized the second. . . . What is the force

> that holds men back, which prevents them from letting go of what they would like to let go? It is the middle-of-the-way anxiety. It is the deprivation, the void in which they are going to find themselves before being able to seize a new support.
>
> We must always be letting go . . . leaving one place in order to find another, abandoning one support in order to reach another, turning our backs on the past in order to thrust wholeheartedly toward the future.[10]

What all people who move have in common is the fact that it is hard to let go of the old, challenging to take hold of the new, and frustrating to be suspended between the two.

Letting Go

One of the hardest parts about moving is what we must leave behind . . . and consequently the things of which we must let go—like the old house. Church trustees are notorious for not maintaining the parsonage. I've known of pastors who are happy to move out of a house that has been inadequate, especially if they're moving to a better, more spacious one that has been kept in good repair.

Still, think of the Christmases you spent in the old house. And the birthdays you celebrated. Maybe it was the first home for one or more of your children. Maybe it wasn't such a great house, but it had a big yard, which was a bonus. Memories are wrapped up in houses. That last pause at the end of the driveway as you're leaving often finds more than one family member shedding a sentimental tear at leaving the old house.

Harder still is leaving old friends. Relationships—that's what a pastorate is all about. Children make friends. Spouses become attached to special people in the congregation. Say all you want about treating everyone the same and not getting too close to the congregation, you will really miss some people. Not having them in your life on a regular basis will be a big adjustment.

What about your old familiar routines? The same route to the office each day. The familiarity of the grocery store. Why, you could almost shop for groceries blindfolded. You know what's on each aisle. Especially if it's a small town, you get to know the cashiers at the store, the tellers at the bank, the owner of the coffee shop. Leaving those things behind is likely to initiate a grieving process.

Grabbing On

Once you get to your new parish, you have many adjustments to make. Besides having a church full of new faces, you and your family have to learn lots of new things. What time does the mail carrier pick up the mail? Whom do you contact about trash pickup? Who can recommend a new doctor? A new dentist? What's the best place to buy your groceries? To buy gas for your car? And what about a mechanic you can trust? Whom do you call to get all the utilities started in your name?

Where will the kids go to school? Where will you turn for a new barber or hair stylist? What's the best place to do your banking? Where is the closest library? It seems like there's no end to the new things that have to be cared for within a reasonable period of time after you land in a new place.

Suspended Between

And believe it or not, some things are simply suspended for the time being. Until this transition is complete, you don't want to cancel your credit cards until you have established new accounts. And maybe even then, depending on the interest rate, you may want to hang on to an old one indefinitely.

Don't cancel your cell phone right away. It may take several days to get a new phone connected if you use a land line. Meanwhile, how will people reach you? Hopefully you have Internet access you can use in your new location until you're sure you have your new computer hooked up and everything is running smoothly. With a laptop or a smart phone, you may not have to worry about being out of touch. But these are things you may hold in suspension for awhile.

And don't forget your breath! You may be holding that occasionally until you settle in to your new routine. How will things go in your new parish? How long until your new congregants trust you? How long until your spouse is content with a new routine? How long until the kids are happy with school and friends?

Three Choices

"What lies behind us and what lies before us are tiny matters compared to what lies within us."

—Ralph Waldo Emerson[11]

You're on the trapeze. You're trying to let go, you're going to grab hold, but right now, you're suspended between the two. But relax; there is a net. It's called the grace of God. You will make the transition. You will eventually grab hold. Through it all, "he gives us more grace" (James 4:6).

Impact on Your Family

Whether you and our family are looking forward to the new church or disappointed you have to leave the old one, there are some important things to remember.

Understand There Will Be an Impact

For positive or negative, for good or bad, there will be an impact on your family.

Most married couples realize sooner or later that they don't make decisions in the same way and they don't make them at the same speed. I have a friend who makes decisions quickly and his wife is more deliberate in her decision making.

He is the pastor and across the years, when they have changed churches, although they discussed the decision, he would come to a conclusion sooner than she would. He would not only make the decision, but he would accept the decision sooner than she. Part of this is because she felt the tug of relationships in the church more keenly than he did. She thought more deeply about the impact on the family than he did.

At the end of the day, however, they always came together and agreed on the decision. His quickness tended to speed her up a bit, and her hesitation tended to slow him down. This was generally a good thing, because it forced him to think things through more deeply than he might have done otherwise.

Take into Account the Differences in Children

All children, whatever their age, will be impacted by your move from one church to another. But they will not all be affected in the same way.

A colleague told me how his third-grade son handled their impending move. The family had discussed the possibility and left it hanging—a move across the country to a different church was possible. They agreed not to talk with others about it; this was strictly a family matter.

In children's church, the leader asked the children for prayer requests. Jeff, the third-grader, raised his hand and said, "Please pray for my dad. He has a big decision to make."

The children's church director, nobody's fool, immediately suspected what that decision was about, but said nothing. A person of integrity, she kept her suspicions to herself. Only after my colleague had decided to move and had announced the decision to the church did the children's church leader come to him. With a shy smile, she told him about Jeff's prayer request.

I have known teens who were elated and excited about moving to a new community. I have known others, like Mitch and Christine in the stories earlier in this chapter, who were devastated at the thought of leaving their friends and moving to a strange place.

Pastor Bob sat down with his children, who were young adults and living in the community, and talked with them about his impending move across the country. A church in a distant state had called him to be their pastor. It would mean a long-distance separation for their family, since there would be no reason for these young people, who had jobs in the community, to relocate with him.

Knowing his decision would impact their lives, he was pleased when they responded, "Dad, we know you have always tried to live your life according to God's will. If this is what he wants you to do, he will work out all the details for both you and us. Go for it!"

Listen to Your Family

Whatever ages your children are and whatever the decision-making process of your family looks like, the important thing is to listen to your spouse and children. Especially if they are upset about the move.

The temptation is to try to solve their problems. Resist that temptation and just listen attentively.

Roots and Wings

Our children need two things: roots and wings.

—author unknown

Listening, caring, understanding, giving people a chance to vent if that's what they need—these are your best tools in helping your family through an impending move. You may be able to point out some distinct advantages in relocating. But don't speak too quickly. You're about to change their lives, and they need to know you care about how this will impact them.

God Works It Out for Our Good

Mitch settled into his sophomore year and did well as a student. He was slow to make friends. He didn't talk much about it, but he missed his buddies that stayed behind in their old church.

Eighteen months later, during the summer before his senior year, he seemed to accept the new school. He went out for football. Although the team didn't win many games, he enjoyed the camaraderie of the players and coaches. After college, in fact, he came back to that town he was so disappointed in moving to several years earlier. He settled down there, got a job, married, and reared his kids in that town.

Christine, in spite of her anger over the long, dreaded move, settled in and made friends. One special friend was the young man who became her husband—and who became a pastor and was responsible for several more moves in her life.

Not all pastors' families have positive stories to tell about their moves. But it is amazing how God works all things for our good. As the poet said: God knows, he loves, he cares. Nothing this truth can dim. He gives his very best to those who leave the choice to him.[12]

Action Steps

1. Think through what would be the greatest impact on your family if you moved within the next twelve months. How would you prepare them to face these changes?
2. In Paul Tournier's example of the trapeze artist, where are you in the process—hanging on, grabbing hold, or suspended? What's your next move?

10

Beginning
Leading During the First Ninety Days

In life, as well as in a new congregation, you never get a second chance to make a good first impression.

In pastoral work, most mistakes can be corrected. Not so with beginnings; I cannot begin at a congregation twice.
—Robert Kemper

Pastor Tom and his wife drove into town slightly ahead of the moving van. They barely had time to unlock the door and take a walk through the parsonage before the van pulled up in front of the house. Once the workers unloaded all the furniture, his wife, Julie, said, "We'd better find a supermarket or we'll starve to death. That's a nice refrigerator in the kitchen, but it's empty."

"Have any idea where the nearest supermarket is?" Tom asked.

"I think I saw one out on the highway a block or two before we turned off into our subdivision. We just need a few things to get us by until I can make some inquiries and find out where is the best place to shop."

They bought their groceries and spent the next couple of days getting boxes unpacked, furniture arranged, pictures hung, and the house in some semblance of order before Sunday arrived.

Their parishioners were very kind and arranged a lovely meal for them after church. They began to get acquainted and felt they were off to a good start before heading back to the parsonage.

Empty nesters now, they had left all their family some eight hundred miles away when they agreed to come to this church. On Monday morning, Tom went to the church office. Much to his surprise, the secretary was on vacation. She always went at this time every year, as she and her husband loved to rent a cabin in the mountains and this was when it was available. She had arranged for a substitute, who knew how to answer the phone, but little else.

Tom had come from a thriving church with multiple staff. He was well-known in the previous community and the church bustled with activity. Something was always happening and it had been the high point in his ministry up until now. This new church had tons of potential, but this was summer and lots of people were gone. In another couple of weeks, parishioners told him, the church would be bursting with college students from the nearby university. They loved the contemporary worship.

Because so many students attended during the school year, the church's budget was much lower than Tom had thought it would be. The students were wonderful and added a lively dimension to the church, but they had no money. Thus, the church operated with a bare-bones staff: the senior pastor, the secretary, and a part-time worship leader, who only came into the church one afternoon a week.

Sitting at his new desk with a substitute secretary stationed in the outer office, Tom had never felt so lonely in his life.

Emotions in a New Pastorate

Loneliness is only one emotion a pastor may feel at the beginning of a new pastorate. Leith Anderson points out some other emotions to which a pastor may fall prey.[1]

Guilt Feelings

In Anderson's case, it was his first pastorate and he felt guilty about not working afternoons. He worked in his study in the mornings and attended church meetings in the evening. With his parishioners at work, he had no one to visit, so he caught up on his reading (or the soap operas) in the afternoon. He could have eliminated the guilt if it had occurred to him that he didn't have to work from 7:00 a.m. until 11:00 p.m.

It does bring up the trap that many pastors fall into in their first pastorate, especially in rural areas. That is feeling the need or the obligation to visit every family in the church. In recent years, pastoral visitation has become less popular. People are busy and most don't want the pastor to drop in unannounced. Many pastors find it difficult even to make appointments, either because people don't want a visit or are too busy.

Those who do try to visit every family will soon find they can't keep it up. As the church grows, more and more demands clamor for the pastor's attention. If a pastor sets the expectation at the outset that regular visitation will be the pattern, resentment may set in later when it becomes impossible to maintain that schedule.

Desire to Be Accepted

Anderson also mentions that when we desire strongly to be liked and accepted, we may be tempted to become like our parishioners. For instance, there may be an expectation to give altar calls at the end of each service. If that works for you and is consistent with your style, fine. But if not, it will be artificial and may, in the long run, make it more difficult for people to respond to the gospel.

Don't be surprised if somebody approaches you about visiting the elderly members, cloaking it with the idea that pastoral visitation is one of the pastor's responsibilities. This tends to suggest you are neglecting your duties and it pushes a guilt trip in your direction. No pastor should neglect congregational care, so that base has to be covered one way or another, either by you, by other staff members, or by sensitive, trained laypersons. But unless you are especially gifted in pastoral care, beware of the temptation to do it out of a sense of obligation, just because you want people to like you.

Eagerness to Succeed

Everyone wants to be successful. But who defines success? Is it the congregation? There you will find about as many different definitions for success as you have members. Depending on their viewpoint, success may be a growing Sunday school, a thriving youth group, a dynamic pulpit ministry, or a bulging bank account in the church's name.

Does your denominational supervisor define success for you? That presents another whole set of hoops to jump through. What about the voice in your head? Is it the subtle voice of your father, who was super-successful at his business?

Coupled with the eagerness to succeed may be the fear of failing. They often go together.

Fear of Inadequacy

In the senior pastor's absence, Shelley's friends expected the assistant pastor to call on her at the hospital when she learned she had an inoperable brain tumor. When he did not go the first day nor the second, someone asked him about it. He blurted, "Seminary did not prepare me to deal with this!"

Soft Skills

"What people get admired and appreciated for in community are their soft skills: their sense of humor and timing, their ability to listen, their courage and honesty, their capacity for empathy."

—M. Scott Peck[2]

Bible college and seminary don't prepare us for a lot of things. They can't. There's not room in the curriculum for every problem you may face. Life prepares us and, even more importantly, the Lord prepares us for what we have to face. In our own strength, none of us is adequate. We find our adequacy in him.

Ninety Days to Get into Trouble

Ninety days. Three months. Thirteen weeks. Not much time. Yet plenty of time to get into big trouble.

Kings Who Got into Trouble

Two kings of Judah served only three months each. Jehoahaz became king when he was twenty-three years old after the tragic death of his father, Josiah, one of the few kings who "did what was right in the eyes of the Lord and walked in all the ways of his father David" (2 Kings 22:2). Unlike his father, Jehoahaz "did evil in the eyes of the Lord" (2 Kings 23:32). We have no other record of anything he did, only the disastrous results.

Pharaoh Neco, king of Egypt, captured him, put him in chains, and took him to Egypt, where he died. Then the Egyptian monarch proceeded to levy a heavy tax on the people of Judah.

Jehoiachin was the other king who reigned only three months. He became king at the age of eighteen. King Nebuchadnezzar of Babylon swooped in and deposed him. The Babylonian army laid siege to the city of Jerusalem, and Nebuchadnezzar himself entered and accepted the surrender of Jehoiachin, his mother, his attendants, his nobles, and all his officials (2 Kings 24:10–11).

Nebuchadnezzar plundered the temple and the palace, confiscating all the treasures and the gold. He took thousands of people captive, including all the officers and fighting men, the artisans and craftsmen, leaving only the poorest people to occupy Jerusalem.

Jehoiachin's end was much happier than Jehoahaz's. Although the former stayed in captivity for nearly four decades, he was finally released from prison. A new king in Babylon, a man named Evil-Merodach, spoke kindly to Jehoiachin, gave him a seat of honor, a generous allowance, and allowed him to eat at the king's table for the rest of his life (2 Kings 25:27–30).

Two kings, ninety days each, and both brought disaster on themselves, their families, and on Judah. God forbid that any pastor be led away in chains after only three months of ministry!

A Trouble-Prone Apostle

Three months were sufficient for the apostle Paul to get into trouble as well. On his third missionary journey, he entered the city of Ephesus and found some disciples who needed instruction about the Holy Spirit. Paul taught them, baptized them in the name of Jesus, and the Holy Spirit came on them (Acts 19:1–6).

That was a good start by anyone's assessment. Yet Paul's good fortune did not last. He entered the synagogue, speaking "boldly, . . . arguing persuasively about the kingdom of God" (Acts 19:8). However, some of the Jews "became obstinate; they refused to believe and publicly maligned the Way" of Christ (Acts 19:9). Paul left the synagogue, took some disciples with him, and moved his ministry to a lecture hall, where he taught for two years.

Most of us would not look kindly on a pastor who comes into town, manages to cause a church split within three months, and starts a competing congregation. But then many churches would not give Paul's resume a second look.

To Paul's credit, during his two years in the lecture hall, "all the Jews and Greeks who lived in the province of Asia heard the word of the Lord" (Acts 19:10).

The apostle had another three-month stint, this time in Greece. Although Dr. Luke does not specify where in Greece he was, it was probably Corinth. Acts records no accomplishments in Corinth during this time, but it was likely here, during the winter of A.D. 55–56 (cf. 1 Cor. 16:6), that he stayed with his "old friend and convert, Gaius (1 Cor. 1:14),"[3] and wrote his letter to the Romans, which he sent by Phoebe (Rom. 16:1–2).

Not that any of us could author a treatise of the same quality as Paul's letter to the Romans, but I would certainly not recommend that any pastor attempt such a feat during the first ninety days in a new parish.

An Effective Ninety Days

Paul's third ninety-day experience involved a deadly snake, a hospitable official, and a mass healing campaign. On his way to Rome, his ship wrecked on a sandbar and the passengers survived by swimming or floating to the nearby island of Malta.

Once on shore, the natives built a fire. As Paul gathered brushwood and added it to the fire, a snake slithered out and fastened itself to his hand. When the islanders saw the snake dangling from his hand, they assumed he was a criminal and fate, allowing him to escape the shipwreck, nevertheless determined to kill him by the viper. When Paul did not die as expected, they assumed he was a god.

Publius, a local official, entertained the ship's company with great hospitality. On learning that his host's father was sick in bed, Paul prayed for him and the man was healed. The rest of the island's sick population came to Paul and he prayed for them too. God honored his faith and healed them all (Acts 27:27—28:10).

This brief period of ministry commends itself to us as a model for ministry. Without God's intervention, Paul might have died from the snakebite. Without God's favor, we are not likely to accomplish anything worthwhile during the first ninety days or at any other time in our ministry.

When Paul found a ministry opportunity—Publius' sick father—he became pastoral and ministered to the man. God honored him again by healing the man and consequently the islanders who were ill.

We cannot depend on miracles to salvage our early days of ministry. Yet as we minister faithfully and as God blesses, we may be surprised at what we can accomplish during the first three months in a new place.

Focus on the Right Things

I have read that most people will change jobs an average of five to seven times during their lifetime and even change careers three to five times.[4] I know that pastors do change churches every few years. Some denominations tend to have longer tenures for their pastors than others, but most pastors change churches three or more times during their career. As Doug Scott says, "Only circus stars move more."[5]

During the first ninety days, you don't have time to do everything. So you must get it right. You must focus on the right things and maximize this short window of opportunity to lead a new congregation.

Build Mutual Trust

One of the best things you can do is to build trust. This takes time and there are few shortcuts you can take. Robert Kemper tells about one minister who began his new pastorate, fresh from a stint as a military chaplain. Armed with his military protocol, he "took command" and began issuing orders. His congregation, not seeing themselves as his own personal battalion, became hostile. They did not trust him. In less than a year, he was "relieved of his command."[6]

Most congregations are prepared to trust their new pastor. Unless they have had an extremely bad experience with a pastor who proved unworthy of their trust, they are willing to give you the benefit of the doubt. Having said that, don't expect them to open up to you about their deepest, most troubling problems the first week you are on the job. You will have to earn their trust.

Often greater trust comes when you lead the congregation through some crisis. This may not occur during your first ninety days. Then again, it may. When my friend's church caught on fire shortly after he arrived (see chapter 5), it became a test of his leadership

During the days that followed, he had to negotiate with a nearby school to rent their auditorium. Since they could only use the auditorium and restrooms—no classrooms—and not wanting to suspend Sunday school during this time, he arranged for portable classrooms. He also set up temporary office space nearby for him and his staff. His efficiency in handling it, along

Most Trusted Professions

In *The Harris Poll*, conducted by telephone with more than one thousand adults between July 7 and 10, 2006, doctors and teachers are the most trusted professions to tell the truth (85 percent and 83 percent, respectively). Rounding out the top five are scientists (77 percent), police officers (76 percent), and professors (75 percent). The bottom five were actors, lawyers, stockbrokers, trade union leaders, and opinion pollsters, ranging from 26 percent to 34 percent. Clergy or priests had actually increased ten percentage points to 74 percent since 2002.[7]

with appropriate compassion for those who felt the loss of their church building until workers could clean and repair the facilities, strengthened his credibility with the congregation.

Introduce Yourself

Most new pastors have meetings where they are asked to tell a little bit about themselves, what their hobbies and interests are, and what they're looking forward to in the new community. Pastors can also find other ways to introduce themselves to the congregation.

The primary way pastors communicate with their congregations is through preaching, which is, of course, truth communicated through personality. While the emphasis must always be more about the truth than about the personality, you will expose your temperament in your preaching. In addition, you might consider a series on basic beliefs as a way to introduce the congregation to your thinking on the fundamentals of the faith.

People Business

"Anyone who doesn't get along with people doesn't belong in this business, because that's all we've got around here."

—Lee Iacocca[8]

One word of caution: Be very careful about using illustrations from your previous parish. What worked there may not work here. What communicated there may or may not communicate here. As tempting as it is to fall back on the familiar, you will want to find illustrations that connect you with your new congregation.

A friend of mine used an illustration about fox hunting in one parish. A member kindly pointed out after the sermon that people in those parts were more familiar with hound dogs and 'coon hunting. That revealed something about both personalities.

Get to Know Them

Over the first three months, you will want to get acquainted with as many people as possible. One way to do this is to invite parishioners into your home. It does not have to be an elaborate affair; dessert and coffee may work well. It gives people an opportunity to see you outside the pulpit and it gives you a chance to get to know them better.

Besides enjoying refreshments together, you may want to ask certain questions, designed to draw people out, to tell you about themselves, but also their stories about the church. Many people are uncomfortable if the questions probe for personal information. So questions about the church and its history, their favorite memories, or high points in the life of the church, may get them to open up to you. This not only acquaints you with the church's history, but it also lets you know what they value.

If having them in your home is not feasible, a gathering at the church, limited to ten or twelve people at a time—twenty at the most, so you can facilitate good conversation—may be the way to accomplish this. Afternoon teas, morning brunches, as well as evening desserts may help to meet the needs of more people.

Another way to get acquainted is to visit people at work, if this is feasible. You may let them know you would like to do this, if possible, and leave it to them to extend an invitation. One pastor visited his parishioners in a variety of places—a shoe repair shop, a hardware store, even a funeral home—and forged meaningful friendships with those who worked in these places.

Celebrations of all kinds are good ways to bring people together, and thus give you opportunities to enjoy fellowship with a variety of people—all with an eye toward getting better acquainted.

By working at it conscientiously, it's amazing how many people you can get to know in ninety days' time—and build trust in the process.

Tips for Getting Settled

People will be anxious to help you get settled—if you ask. They may be cautious about coming forward and volunteering information. But if you ask for help, most people will give it.

Ask for Help

On the rare occasions when I have overcome my manly pride and asked for directions, most people were eager to help. I haven't always been able to understand their directions, but I had to admire their enthusiasm and their willingness to help.

One pastor, prior to moving to the new community, asked the congregation if they would think about the things they discovered when first arriving in that community. He asked them to think about their favorite places or pieces of information.

He reported that the response was overwhelming. They wrote down and gave the pastor information on everything from the best hardware store to good picnic spots, to telephone numbers for all kinds of things. Some gave the names of good babysitters or offered themselves to babysit. Others simply gave their own phone number and urged the new pastor to call anytime. It was the kind of information that might have taken the pastor and his family months to dig up on their own.[9]

Such an open invitation makes an immediate connection between the pastor and his congregation. When people help you, they feel drawn to you.

Taking Advice

"There are two quick ways to disaster: taking nobody's advice and taking everybody's advice."

—author unknown

Visiting Everyone

What about visitation? Times have changed. Most congregations no longer expect—and many do not want—the pastor to visit them. How will you know what to do, what's expected, and how you should respond?

One suggestion is to put the ball in their court. You could say something like, "I am interested in getting better acquainted with everyone in the congregation. But I don't know your schedules and I'm pretty sure you don't want me to show up at your door unexpectedly. So if you would like me to make a home visit, please contact me and let me know a good time for me to visit. I will do my best to work out a schedule that fits both you and me."

Sometimes pastors hear from parishioners that they don't visit enough. If you have made the above offer to your congregation, and if someone complains about your lack of visitation, you can remind them of your policy. You can ask, "Have you called to invite me? I would be happy to come. Just let me know when it's a good time for you and your family."

Be Cautious about Making Changes

I have heard "experts" give contrary advice on making changes in a new pastorate. Some will say, "Be careful and don't change anything for the first year you are there. Focus on getting acquainted and find out all you can about the church before you begin to make changes."

Others say, "You will have a window of opportunity when you first arrive in a new parish, when people will expect you to make changes. After all, you are the new leader and they expect you to lead differently from your predecessor."

Supernatural Change

"If you want others to 'buy in' to change, start with this reality check: Change is naturally an imposition to human beings. Then begin with this teaching: Change is supernaturally at the center of what God does. When he set the earth in motion, he created a world of change."

—Kent Hunter[10]

There is wisdom in both pieces of advice—and potential snares as well. You will have a window of opportunity when you can make some changes. But I do not advise you to make major changes unless you have no other choice. If your worship leader moves away or walks out the first Sunday, you will have to find someone else. That is potentially a big change, depending on the worship styles of the departing and arriving musicians.

Taking time to listen and to learn what some of the sacred cows are may keep you from stumbling into the meat grinder and making hamburger of yourself. Every church has its idiosyncrasies and you will not know all of these when you first arrive. So advance cautiously with your antennae up and using your best spiritual discernment. If at all possible, secure the advice and support of the lay leaders in the church before making changes.

Make Yourself at Home

Pastor Tom's loneliness didn't last long. When school started and the students returned, their youthful enthusiasm once again pervaded the atmosphere.

Whatever the circumstances are when you arrive in your new assignment, just settle in and feel at home. A colleague from my home state of West Virginia told about his mother asking him one day, "Of all the places you've lived, doesn't West Virginia seem more like home?"

"Well, Mom," he answered, "I don't want to hurt your feelings, but in my line of work, it's important to settle down where you are, learn to love the people, and make yourself at home."

His answer parallels Jeremiah's advice to the people in exile: "Build houses and settle down; plant gardens and eat what they produce. . . . Also, seek the peace and prosperity of the city to which I have carried you into exile. Pray to the Lord for it, because if it prospers, you too will prosper" (Jer. 29:5, 7).

Even though you're not in exile, invest yourself in your new congregation and community. With God's blessing, your tenure will be long and fruitful.

Action Steps

1. Make a list of information you want your new congregation to provide for you.
2. Discuss with your spouse what you can do to get acquainted with your new parishioners. Agree on a strategy for the first ninety days.

Appendix A

Pastor-to-Pastor Debrief Checklist

A departing pastor can help his or her successor a great deal by taking advantage of a face-to-face conversation, in which, without criticism of the congregation, the departing pastor shares information with the new pastor.

Pastoral Oversight

- Names of shut-ins
- Names of terminally ill
- Names of bereaved in last twelve months
- Patterns of pastoral care
- Unusual expectations of pastor
- Who is angry at the church or pastor?
- Who are important allies?
- Who has broken trust?
- Who has an agenda?
- Who will keep confidences?
- Who is sexually aggressive?
- Who is in danger of burning out?
- Who is underused?
- Who are the five most influential persons in the church?

Worship

- Traditions and styles
- Attendance trends
- Recent controversies
- Preaching style
- Seasonal variations
- Special services

Program

- Master list of programs
- Fundraising approaches
- Giving patterns and records
- Adult spiritual formation
- Child and youth spiritual formation
- New programs that need support
- Older programs that are still vital
- Seasonal traditions

Administration

- Role of board
- Committee structure
- Meeting cycles
- Annual program calendar
- Financial trends and issues
- Report formats
- Facility issues and policies
- Keys and access issues
- Alarm system

Personnel

- Staff structure
- Job descriptions

- Evaluation process
- Staff meetings and agenda
- Recent hires and terminations
- Training and coaching
- Confidentiality

Church Climate

- How warm are church members to one another? To new people?
- How is the morale in this church?
- How open is this church to change?
- What are the significant conflicts in the church?
- How central is faith to members' lives?
- How conservative or liberal is this church?
- How diverse is this church theologically, ethnically, and demographically?
- Where are the landmines?
- Who are the saints?

Other

____

____

____

—Adapted from Caroly Weese and J. Russell Crabtree, *The Elephant in the Boardroom* (San Fransico: Jossey-Bass, 2004), 153–154.

Appendix B

Interview Questions

In your candidating interview, prepare a list of questions to give you a sense of the committee members' attitudes and expectations. The questions could include these:

1. Why am I of particular interest to you?
2. What has been the most significant event in the life of this congregation since you have been a member?
3. Aside from the upheaval of looking for a new pastor, what has been the most upsetting event in the life of this church?
4. In your opinion, what areas of concern need to be addressed by this congregation?
5. What kinds of things did your former pastor do particularly well?
6. What were the circumstances surrounding your former pastor's departure?
7. In what areas did you wish your former pastor had more expertise?
8. What formal and informal methods of support have you used in the past to help your pastor become a better minister?
9. Tell me about the governing board.

10. Has the pastor's family traditionally taken an active role in the church?
11. How is the pastor's compensation package determined? How frequently is it reviewed? By whom? What factors are used in determining that package? Merit or cost-of-living increases? Social Security reimbursement? Equity in the parsonage or a cash equity allowance? Continuing education, book, and automobile allowances?
12. How should your pastor spend his or her time? In the course of a week, how much time should be spent in prayer? Personal study? Sermon preparation? Administration? Individual and family counseling? Visiting? With the family?
13. What organizations in the congregation are the most active or successful?
14. Beyond calling a pastor and its related concerns, what is the highest congregational priority for the next twelve months?
15. What goals have you established for church growth? What methods can be used to achieve those goals?
16. What plans have you made for the expansion of staff or buildings?
17. How financially stable is this congregation?
18. What programs do you plan to implement in the next ten years?

—Adapted from Douglas Scott, "Getting the Real Story," in Ed Bratcher, Robert Kemper, and Douglas Scott, *Mastering Transitions* (Portland, Ore.: Multnomah, 1991), 29ff.

NOTES

Chapter 1

1. Seth Borenstein, "NASA Chief's Wife to Obama: Don't Fire My Husband," *USA Today*, December 31, 2008, http://www.usatoday.com/tech/science/space/2008-12-31-nasa-chief-wife_N.htm (accessed May 28, 2009).
2. John Drescher, "If I Were Starting My Ministry Again," cited in *Current Thoughts and Trends*, March 1996, 14.
3. Quoted in *U.S. News & World Report*, April 3, 2006, 18.
4. Robert V. Remini, *John Quincy Adams* (New York: Times Books, 2002), 118ff.
5. Michael Burlingame, *The Inner World of Abraham Lincoln* (Urbana, Ill.: University of Illinois Press, 1994), 193–194.
6. From author's file; no other attribution available.
7. Jeff Mansell, *Teammates*, September 2002, 1.
8. Lloyd Ogilvie, *The Communicator's Commentary: Acts* (Dallas: Word, 1983), 242.
9. Cited by John Stott, *The Spirit, the Church, and the World: The Message of Acts* (Downers Grove, Ill.: InterVarsity Press, 1990), 258.
10. Charles W. Carter and Ralph Earle, *The Evangelical Commentary on The Acts of the Apostles* (Grand Rapids, Mich.: Zondervan, 1959), 229.
11. Chuck Swindoll, "Model the Master," *Stimulus*, Spring 1996, 1–2.
12. Bobb Biehl, e-mail, *Quick Wisdom*, August 30, 2007.
13. Bob Kobielush, "Thinking With Your Gut," *Executive Briefing*, January 2003, 1.

Chapter 2

1. Cited by John Ortberg, *If You Want to Walk on Water, You've Got to Get Out of the Boat* (Grand Rapids, Mich.: Zondervan, 2001), 61–63.
2. Stuart Briscoe, Knute Larson, and Larry Osborne, *Measuring Up* (Sisters, Ore.: Multnomah, 1993), 18.
3. Todd Gaddis, "But the Grass is So Green," *Focus on the Family*, December 2002, 10–11.

4. Keith Drury, "Why in the World Would a Super Church Pastor Leave?" www.TuesdayColumn.com, http://www.drurywriting.com/keith/superch.htm (accessed June 14, 2009).
5. Craig Brian Larson, *Pastoral Grit* (Minneapolis: Bethany House Publishers, 1998), 101.
6. Stewart Pierson, "Keys to a Long Pastorate," *Leadership*, Spring 1984, 136.
7. Leith Anderson, Jack Hayford, and Ben Patterson, *Who's in Charge?* (Sisters, Ore.: Multnomah, 1993), 95.
8. Briscoe, Larson, and Osborne, 17–18.
9. Eugene H. Peterson, *The Contemplative Pastor* (Dallas: Word, 1989), 57.
10. Stuart Briscoe, *The Communicator's Commentary: Genesis* (Waco, Tex.: Word, 1987), 173.
11. Cited by John Maxwell, *The Communicator's Commentary: Deuteronomy* (Waco, Tex.: Word, 1987), 321.
12. Rob Portlock, *Leadership*, Summer 1986, 79.
13. Lynn Anderson, "Why I've Stayed," *Leadership*, Summer 1986, 78–79.
14. From author's file; no other attribution available.
15. Bobb Biehl, *Dream Energy* (USA: Quick Wisdom Publishing, 2001), 5.
16. From author's file; no other attribution available.
17. John Mason, *An Enemy Called Average* (Tulsa: Honor Publishing, 1993).
18. Ortberg, 63.

Chapter 3

1. Jimmy Carter, *An Hour Before Daylight* (New York: Simon & Schuster, 2001), 266.
2. Paul B. Meyer, *The Dynamics of Personal Leadership* (Waco, Tex.: Success Motivation Institute, Inc., 1969), 20.
3. Cited in *Success*, November 1996, 14.
4. Don Shula and Ken Blanchard, *Everyone's a Coach* (New York: Harper Business, 1995), 73.
5. Stuart Briscoe, *The Communicator's Commentary: Romans* (Waco, Tex.: Word, 1982), 217.
6. From author's file; no other attribution available.
7. Bill Hybels, "The Art of Self-Leadership," *Leadership*, Summer 2001, 87.
8. John Mason, *An Enemy Called Average* (Tulsa: Honor Publishing, 1993), 222.

9. Hybels, 88.
10. Max Lucado, *Every Day Deserves a Chance* (Nashville: Thomas Nelson, 2007), 99–100.
11. Max Lucado, *He Still Moves Stones* (Dallas: Word, 1993), 78.
12. InterVarsity, "Great Cloud of Witnesses," http://www.urbana.org/great-cloud-of-witnesses/david-livingstone-1813-1873 (accessed June 28, 2009).
13. Cited in *Leadership*, Summer 1994, 114.
14. From author's file; no other attribution available.
15. Stephen Covey, *The Seven Habits of Highly Effective People* (New York: Simon & Schuster, 1989), 43.
16. Everett Lewis Cattell, *The Spirit of Holiness* (Grand Rapids, Mich.: Eerdmans Publishing, 1963), 61–62.
17. Peter Drucker, "Your Leadership is Unique," *Leadership*, Fall 1996, http://www.ctlibrary.com/le/1996/fall/6l4054.html (accessed June 23, 2009).
18. Ibid.
19. From author's file; no other attribution available.
20. "Henry Ford Quotes," http://thinkexist.com/quotes/henry_ford/2.html (accessed July 10, 2009).
21. "Georges Clemenceau Quotes," http://thinkexist.com/quotes/georges_clemenceau (accessed July 10, 2009).
22. Interview with Ben Utecht on *The Hour of Power*, http://www.crystalcathedral.org/hour_of_power/interviews/detail.php?contentid=4097 (accessed June 28, 2009).

Chapter 4

1. Cited by Jerry Clark, http://askax.net/2007/04/03/stop moaning-groaning-whimpering-whining-and-get-result/ (accessed July 19, 2009).
2. Cited by John Mason, *An Enemy Called Average* (Tulsa: Honor Publishing, 1993), 87.
3. Judith Sills, *McCall's*, from author's file; no other attribution available.
4. Cited by John Maxwell, *Failing Forward* (Nashville: Thomas Nelson, 2000), 160.
5. Dean Hoge and Jacqueline Wenger, *Pastor in Transition: Why Clergy Leave Local Church Ministry* (Grand Rapids, Mich.: Eerdmans Publishing, 2005), cited by Dr. Aron Willis in an unpublished seminar, "Weathering Transition: Finding Focus in Ministry Change," The Gathering, Orlando, Fla., January 2007.
6. Philip A. Bence, *Acts: A Bible Commentary in the Wesleyan Tradition* (Indianapolis: Wesleyan Publishing House, 1998), 162–163.

7. Mason, *An Enemy Called Average*, 127–128.
8. Nido R. Qubein, from author's file; no other attribution available.
9. Cited in "Facing Change with Confidence," *Ministry Advantage*, Nov/Dec 1994.
10. Wisdom Quotes, http://www.wisdomquotes.com/002078.html (accessed July 19, 2009).
11. Lewis Smedes, "Forgiving God," *Theology, News and Notes*, June 1996, 12.
12. Edward Grinnan, "Take a Moment . . ." *Guideposts*, July 2009, 2.
13. *Peter Lowe's Success Talk*, vol. 65, with Kurt and Brenda Warner, audiotape, May 2000.
14. Cited by Victor M. Parachin, "Changes," *Aspire*, Dec 1994/Jan 1995, 79.
15. Sheila Murray Bethel, http://www.bethelinstitute.com/downloads/4_ways_to_master_change.pdf (accessed July 19, 2009).
16. "John Maynard Keynes Quotes," http://thinkexist.com/quotes/john_maynard_ keynes (accessed July 19, 2009).
17. Tony Campolo, *Let Me Tell You a Story* (Nashville: Word, 2000), 84.
18. Bethel.
19. University of Maryland Medical Center, http://www.umm.edu/news/releases/laughter.htm (accessed July 19, 2009).
20. Loma Linda Univeristy, http://www.llu.edu/news/today/mar99/sm.htm (accessed July 19, 2009).
21. Wisdom Quotes, http://www.wisdomquotes.com/000238.html (accessed July 19, 2009).
22. From author's file; no other attribution available.

Chapter 5

1. Craig Brian Larson, *Pastoral Grit* (Minneapolis: Bethany House Publishers, 1998), 76.
2. Brian Ray, "Contemplating a Career Change?" http://www.christianitytoday.com/workplace/articles/contemplating careerchange.html (accessed August 6, 2009).
3. Ibid.
4. Henry H. Halley, *Halley's Bible Handbook* (Grand Rapids, Mich.: Zondervan, 1965), 230.
5. George Sweeting, "God Isn't a Quitter," adapted from *Too Soon to Quit* (Chicago: Moody Press, 1999), http://www.christianity today.com/moi/2005/006/november/4.4.html (accessed August 6, 2009).
6. Ibid.

7. Andy Stanley, *Visioneering* (Sisters, Ore.: Multnomah, 1999), 186–187.
8. Stuart Briscoe, *The Communicator's Commentary: Romans* (Waco, Tex.: Word, 1982), 27.
9. David L. McKenna, *Renewing Our Ministry* (Waco, Tex.: Word, 1986), 11.
10. Sweeting.
11. Martha Dunagin Saunders, "3 Words That Can Change Your Life," *Reader's Digest*, February 1994, 137.
12. John Maxwell and Jim Dornan, *Becoming a Person of Influence* (Nashville: Thomas Nelson, 1997), 103.
13. Max Lucado, *Every Day Deserves a Chance* (Nashville: Thomas Nelson, 2007), 5.
14. Marvin Olasky, "Are We Ready?" *World*, May 5, 2007, 44.
15. Bobb Biehl, *Quick Wisdom*, e-mail, January 6, 2009.
16. Jim Collins, *Good to Great* (New York: Harper Business, 2001), 82.
17. Cited by John Maxwell, *Failing Forward* (Nashville: Thomas Nelson, 2000), 143.
18. Cited by Earle L. Wilson, *Holy and Human* (Indianapolis: Wesleyan Publishing House, 2008), 90.

Chapter 6

1. Phil Stevenson, "The Lights Will Go Out," *Expanding Wave: A Missional Resource*, e-mail newsletter, August 19, 2009.
2. J. Oswald Sanders, *Spiritual Leadership*, rev. ed. (Chicago: Moody Press, 1989), 177.
3. John Mason, *An Enemy Called Average* (Tulsa: Honor Publishing 1993), 189.
4. Donald Bubna, "How to Bid a Healthy Farewell," *Leadership*, Summer 1988, 123.
5. James Humes, *Speak Like Churchill, Stand Like Lincoln* (New York: Three Rivers Press, 2002), 92.
6. Marvin Olasky, *The American Leadership Tradition* (Wheaton, Ill.: Crossway Books, 1999), 101–102.
7. Wendy Murray Zoba, "Not Your Father's Evangelist," *Christianity Today*, April 5, 1999, http://www.ctlibrary.com/ct/1999/april5/9t4052.html (accessed August 14, 2009).
8. Timothy C. Morgan, "After the Aloha Shirts," http://www.ctlibrary.com/ct/2008/october/16.42.html (accessed August 14, 2009).
9. "War of the Spanish Succession," Microsoft® Encarta® Online Encyclopedia 2009, http://encarta.msn.com (accessed August 18, 2009).

10. L. L. Barkat, *Stone Crossings* (Downers Grove, Ill.: InterVarsity Press, 2008), cited in http://www.christianitytoday.com/lyris/workplace/archives/03-03-2009.html (accessed August 14, 2009).
11. Bubna, 122.
12. Ibid., 123.

Chapter 7

1. Gary L. McIntosh, "The McIntosh Church Growth Network," October 2002, 2.
2. Douglas Scott, "Getting the Real Story: A Guide to Candidating," in Ed Bratcher, Robert Kemper, and Douglas Scott, *Mastering Transitions* (Portland, Ore.: Multnomah, 1991), 33–34.
3. Richard P. Hansen, "The Sound of Clashing Expectations," *Leadership*, 79.
4. F. F. Bruce, *The Gospel of John* (Grand Rapids, Mich.: Eerdmans Publishing, 1983), 300.
5. Ibid., 301.
6. Cited by Wendy Murray Zoba, "Father, Son, and . . ." *Christianity Today*, June 17, 1996, 22.
7. Scott, "Getting the Real Story," 27–28.
8. "Victor Hugo Quotes," http://www.quotes.net/authors/Victor+Hugo (accessed September 19, 2009).
9. BrainyQuote, http://www.brainyquote.com/quotes/authors/m/miguel_de_cervantes.html (accessed September 19, 2009).
10. From author's file; no other attribution available.

Chapter 8

1. Robert Kemper, "Preparing to Leave," in *Empowering Your Church through Creativity and Change*, ed. Marshall Shelley (Nashville: Moorings, 1995), 295–296.
2. Cited in *Christianity Today*, July 10, 2000, 45.
3. *The Pastor's Weekly Briefing*, December 31, 1999, 1.
4. Knute Larson, "Making the Right Moves," in Stuart Briscoe, Knute Larson, and Larry Osborne, *Measuring Up* (Sisters, Ore.: Multnomah, 1993), 72.
5. Stan Toler, *Stan Toler's Practical Guide for Pastoral Ministry* (Indianapolis: Wesleyan Publishing House, 2007), 267.
6. Max Lucado, *Every Day Deserves a Chance* (Nashville: Thomas Nelson, 2007), 87.
7. Andy Stanley, *Visioneering* (Sisters, Ore.: Multnomah, 1999), 56.
8. Cited in *Leadership*, Fall 1990, 49.

9. "George Washington's Farewell Address to the People of the United States," http://www.earlyamerica.com/earlyamerica/milestones/farewell/ (accessed September 12, 2009).
10. Lucado, *Every Day Deserves a Chance*, 28.
11. Lee Strobel, *God's Outrageous Claims* (Grand Rapids, Mich.: Zondervan, 1997), 133.
12. Ronald Reagan, "Farewell Address to the Nation," http://www.ronaldreagan.com/sp_21.html (accessed September 12, 2009).
13. Wikipedia, "Exit Strategy," http://en.wikipedia.org/wiki/Exit_strategy (accessed September 12, 2009).
14. Orval Butcher, "The Transfer of a Treasure," *Leadership*, Summer 1982, 98–99.
15. Ibid., 99–100.
16. Cited by Jerry B. Jenkins in *Writing for the Soul* (Cincinnati: Writer's Digest Books, 2006), 64.
17. Kemper, "Preparing to Leave," 300.
18. Cited by Richard L. Phillips and Charles R. McConnell, *The Effective Corrections Manager: Correctional Supervision for the Future* (Sudbury, Mass.: Jones and Bartlett, 2004), 47.

Chapter 9

1. Susan Miller, *After the Boxes are Unpacked* (Wheaton, Ill.: Tyndale House Publishers, 1995), 11.
2. Billy Graham, Desk Calendar, April 18, 1995.
3. Cited by Earle L. Wilson, *Holy and Human* (Indianapolis: Wesleyan Publishing House, 2008), 131.
4. *The Pastor's Story File*, November 1993, 1.
5. *NIV Reflecting God Study Bible* (Grand Rapids, Mich.: Zondervan, 2000), 24.
6. Elisabeth Elliot, "The Liberty of Obedience to God," *Preaching Today*, vol. 182, 1998, 3.
7. "Seasonal Affective Disorder," http://www.mayoclinic.com/health/seasonal-affective-disorder/DS00195 (accessed September 16, 2009).
8. Miller, 28.
9. Ibid., 22.
10. Paul Tournier, *A Place for You* (New York: Harper & Row, 1968), 162–164.
11. AumCreations, http://www.aumcreations.com/default_pages/positivequotes.htm (accessed September 19, 2009).
12. Benjamin Malachi Franklin, "The Weaver," http://www.flickr.com/photos/protophotogsl/sets/72157621687715839/ (accessed September 22, 2009).

Chapter 10

1. Leith Anderson, "I'm the Leader, Now What?" in *Renewing Your Church through Vision and Planning*, ed. Marshall Shelley (Minneapolis: Bethany House Publishers, 1997), 16–18.
2. Apple Seeds, http://www.appleseeds.org/Dec_01.htm (accessed September 19, 2009).
3. Charles W. Carter and Ralph Earle, *The Acts of the Apostles* (Grand Rapids, Mich.: Zondervan, 1959), 302–303.
4. Northwestern UCS, "Career Myths," http://www.north western.edu/careers/explorecareers/career/ myths.html (accessed September 21, 2009).
5. Douglas Scott, "Moving Right In," in Ed Bratcher, Robert Kemper, and Douglas Scott, *Mastering Transitions* (Portland, Ore.: Multnomah, 1991), 63.
6. Robert Kemper, "The First Year," in Bratcher, Kemper, and Scott, *Mastering Transitions*, 80.
7. Harris Interactive, http://www.harrisinteractive.com/harris_poll/index.asp?PID=688 (accessed September 21, 2009).
8. Cited by Harvey Mackay, *Swim with the Sharks* (New York: William Morrow, 1988), 44.
9. Scott, "Moving Right In," 64.
10. Kent Hunter, "The Change Challenge," *Rev!*, Sept/Oct 2001.